# Per sepno ne's Chil dren

# Persephone's Children

## a life in fragments

## ROWAN MCCANDLESS

RARE MACHINES

Publisher: Scott Fraser | Acquiring editor: Whitney French
Cover design and illustrations: Laura Boyle | Interior designer: Sophie Paas-Lang
Printer: Marquis Book Printing Inc.

**Library and Archives Canada Cataloguing in Publication**

Title: Persephone's children : a life in fragments / Rowan McCandless.
Names: McCandless, Rowan, 1958- author.
Description: Includes bibliographical references.
Identifiers: Canadiana (print) 20200373374 | Canadiana (ebook) 20200373439 | ISBN
    9781459747616 (softcover) | ISBN 9781459747623 (PDF) | ISBN 9781459747630 (EPUB)
Subjects: LCSH: McCandless, Rowan, 1958- | CSH: Women authors, Canadian (English)—
    21st century—Biography. | LCSH: Abused women—Canada—Biography. | CSH: Black
    Canadian women—Biography. | LCSH: Racially mixed women—Canada—Biography. |
    LCGFT: Autobiographies.
Classification: LCC PS8625.C364 Z46 2021 | DDC C818/.603—dc23

We acknowledge the support of the Canada Council for the Arts and the Ontario Arts Council for our publishing program. We also acknowledge the financial support of the Government of Ontario, through the Ontario Book Publishing Tax Credit and Ontario Creates, and the Government of Canada.

Care has been taken to trace the ownership of copyright material used in this book. The author and the publisher welcome any information enabling them to rectify any references or credits in subsequent editions.

The publisher is not responsible for websites or their content unless they are owned by the publisher.

Printed and bound in Canada.

Rare Machines, an imprint of Dundurn Press
1382 Queen Street East
Toronto, Ontario, Canada M4L 1C9
dundurn.com, @dundurnpress 𝕏 f ⊙

# Contents

We are, I am, you are
by cowardice or courage
the one who find our way
back to this scene
carrying a knife, a camera
a book of myths
in which
our names do not appear.

— Adrienne Rich,
from "Diving into the Wreck"

Blood Tithes: A Primer

**_A_ is for ancestry.**

Those who have come before me. Those who are known. Those who have been lost and will never be found. _A_ is also for ambiguity, anemia, and ancestry.ca.

**_B_ is for blood.**

As in ties, as in relatives, as in covenant.

Blood can boil, run hot, run cold. Blood is thicker than water, according to your father's family creed passed down through generations. Cast adrift on a sea of whiteness, family became your only life preserver.

Blood of the covenant. Blood of the womb.

Another interpretation: The bond between soldiers on the battlefield, forged ties stronger than family.

_B_ is for Black Empire Loyalists, for Black Canadian history neglected, erased, and never taught in school.

Grandma Daisy, your father's mother, was the keeper of family history. "Remember," she said. "You be proud. You're eighth-generation Canadian on your father's side. Our people came up with the Empire Loyalists. We've been here longer than most, and still they treat us like dirt."

*B* is also for brown, for Black, for a colour of crayon, a bullshit concept called "race" — the "one-drop rule" that reigned over wombs for the benefit of white privilege.

### *C* is for conception.

Immaculate, miraculous, or otherwise.

*C* is also for childbirth, and for crabapple — the only species of apple tree native to North America.

Once upon a time, a pregnant woman was tempted by ripe, reddened crabapples hanging from backyard tree branches. She plucked and ate, ate and plucked, until she doubled over in pain and was rushed to the hospital, confusing the agony of labour with a wicked stomach ache. Your mother called you her "crabapple baby," as if your intention since conception was to cause her pain.

Civil rights. Civil wrongs. *C* is for colour, coloured, colouring. First years of elementary school with fresh packs of Crayolas, you had trouble staying within the lines — excited by the prospect of filling mimeographed colouring sheets with tangerine grass, ruby-red raindrops, and aubergine skies.

But you never knew what to do with that "flesh" crayon.

Before,

You were Black,

You were Coloured,

You were caught

In a trap

Not of your choice or creation.

*C* is for Catholicism,

censer,

censor,

and censure.

"We had trouble finding a priest that would marry us," Mother said. "They said it was wrong for a Black man and a white woman to be together."

Your father was in charge of Sunday family drives, while your mother nourished soul as well as body. You rose early in the morning, dressed in your very best for Catholic Mass, your dark hair hidden modestly, apologetically, beneath a babushka, just like your Polish Canadian mother, her mother, her grandmother's mother; Eve's daughters, your bodies wellsprings of original sin. You sat on worn wooden pews next to your mother, next to your brothers, next to families who accepted you and families who didn't. You listened to the liturgy in Latin; sat, stood, kneeled, and genuflected under the watchful eyes of priests, saints in stained-glass windows, statues of the Virgin Mary and of her son nailed to the Cross.

You learned man was made in God's image — a likeness white as driven snow. Father, Son, and the Holy Ghost. You questioned how you fit in without a penis or purity of bloodline.

🝀

**𝒟 is for Dark Shadows.**
The late-sixties/early-seventies black-and-white American goth-ic TV soap opera that scared the bejesus out of you when you were younger. Dark Shadows, a supernatural tale of the Collins family, with witches, ghosts, and vampire curses; Barnabas Collins, released from his coffin with an unquenchable thirst for blood.

For a time, as a child, you believed vampires were real. At night you sought comfort in the rose-coloured plastic crucifix your Grandma Frances had given you. It dangled from a delicate chain around your neck. You slept in bed with the hallway light on, slept on the living room couch with one arm draped across your neck.

*D* is for dolls and dress-up, being "Daddy's little girl" whether you wanted to or not.

*D* is for diasporas across ocean and continents, huddled masses fleeing poverty and persecution in the bowels of ships' steerage, Massa's slaves, shackled in chains, transported in Hell's wooden underbelly.

*D* is for divisions.

Divides                                                         not to be crossed.

*D* is also for divorce.

Your father was always on the run, out on a run, out on a run with the railroad, or with whichever woman currently had his favour.

A train whistle echoed from the railroad tracks a block away from your family's bungalow on Washington Avenue; reminders of father and grandfather, the dirge of men called "boy," carrying the baggage of strangers.

## *E* is for Eucharist.

The body and blood of Christ, a sacrament that filled you momentarily with divine grace as a child, a sacrament that also filled you with trepidation and sorrow for the god who could have sacrificed his son.

## *F* is for First Communion.

The two-by-two procession down the scarlet carpeted aisle of St. Alphonsus Church. Boys in suits. Girls in virginal white layers of satin, tulle, and lace, floral headbands and matching veils. Your souls were wed to Christ.

*F* is for fathers, lost and found, founders of colonization, Confederation, and genocide.

*Rowan's First Communion*    *Rowan's Communion processional*

*First row, second from left, Rowan's Auntie Addie*

The Aryan races will not wholesomely amalgam-
ate with the Africans.... [T]he cross of those
races, like the cross of the dog and the fox, is not
successful; it cannot be, and never will be."

— Sir John A. Macdonald, House of Commons debate, 1885

*F* is for father, our father, your father, the holy ghost who left
more times than you can remember.

*G* is for genesis.

The legacy of blood lines — cut and bruised, black and blue …

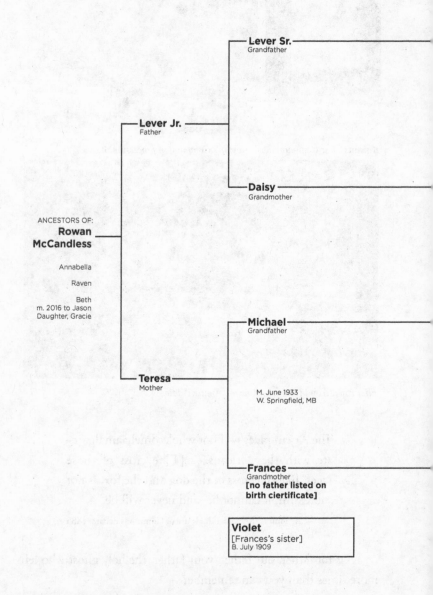

ANCESTORS OF:
**Rowan McCandless**

Annabella

Raven

Beth
m. 2016 to Jason
Daughter, Gracie

**Lever Jr.**
Father

**Lever Sr.**
Grandfather

**Daisy**
Grandmother

**Teresa**
Mother

**Michael**
Grandfather

M. June 1933
W. Springfield, MB

**Frances**
Grandmother
**[no father listed on birth ciertificate]**

**Violet**
[Frances's sister]
B. July 1909

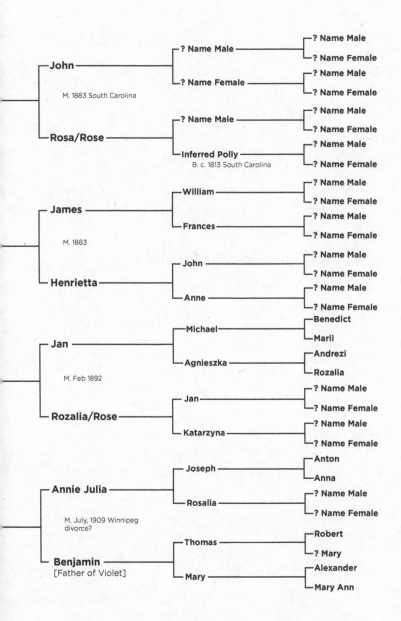

John ── M. 1883 South Carolina
- ? Name Male
  - ? Name Male
    - ? Name Male
    - ? Name Female
  - ? Name Female
    - ? Name Male
    - ? Name Female
- Rosa/Rose
  - ? Name Male
    - ? Name Male
    - ? Name Female
  - Inferred Polly — B. c. 1813 South Carolina
    - ? Name Male
    - ? Name Female

James ── M. 1883
- William
  - ? Name Male
  - ? Name Female
- Frances
  - ? Name Male
  - ? Name Female
- Henrietta
  - John
    - ? Name Male
    - ? Name Female
  - Anne
    - ? Name Male
    - ? Name Female

Jan ── M. Feb 1892
- Michael
  - Benedict
  - Marii
- Agnieszka
  - Andrezi
  - Rozalia
- Rozalia/Rose
  - Jan
    - ? Name Male
    - ? Name Female
  - Katarzyna
    - ? Name Male
    - ? Name Female

Annie Julia ── M. July, 1909 Winnipeg divorce?
- Joseph
  - Anton
  - Anna
- Rosalia
  - ? Name Male
  - ? Name Female
- Benjamin [Father of Violet]
  - Thomas
    - Robert
    - ? Mary
  - Mary
    - Alexander
    - Mary Ann

Generations stolen from Africa.

*G* is for grands and greats.

*Grandpa Mike's parents, Jan and Rosie*

*Grandma Frances's family in Canada*

*Grandma Daisy and Grandpa Lever*

*Grandma Frances, Grandpa Mike, and Aunt Vee*

Genesis 3:16: "Unto the woman, God said, I will greatly multiply thy sorrow and thy conception; in sorrow thou shalt bring forth children."

Grade six health class. The girls were sequestered in the classroom for "the talk," seated behind desks, blinds drawn, door closed. Keep out — no boys allowed! The screen rattled as it was lowered in front of the blackboard. The projector motor hummed and the film reel spun, *clickclickclick*. Dust motes floated in front of the projector's beam while you froze — caught in the headlights — and bore witness to sloughed cells and sterile, anatomical line drawings explaining menstruation. You heard the recess crack of baseball bats, the whoop and holler of boys at play, and longed to join them.

Your mother called menstruation "the curse." She purchased cumbersome boxes of Kotex kept hidden from view behind Bendersky's grocery counter.

The day you started bleeding, you were walking home from junior high school. Blood stained white leotards, white cotton panties. You rushed home and dialed your mother at work. She returned with a box of sanitary pads the size of pillows, an elastic belt to hold them in place, and the following pronouncement: "Be careful," she said. "You could have a baby now." Which left you confused. At twelve, you had yet to kiss a boy and were far more interested in riding your bike, reading books, and playing baseball.

*H* is for hypodescent.

Hypodescent: the assignment of "mixed-race" children to the subordinate group by the dominant culture.

Hyperdescent: the assignment of "mixed-race" children to the more-advantaged group by the dominant culture.

Hit and miss: whether you're perceived as Black, white, or somewhere in between a rock and a hard place.

***I* is for immigration.**

> Up to April 10, 1978, to talk of racism *in* Canadian immigration policy is over generous to the Government of Canada. Rather we should talk of racism *as* Canadian immigration policy.
>
> — David Matas

Fuelled by British Imperialism, after the genocide of First Nations people on the Prairies, Canada sought to repopulate the West. The desirability of new arrivals was rated as follows: immigrants from Great Britain and the United States, northern and western Europeans, central and eastern Europeans, Jews and southern Europeans, pacifist religious sects. Black and Asian immigrants need not apply.

Descendants of peasants, of serfs tied to the land and to landowners who ruled over their lives from birth to grave, your mother's family was part of the first two waves of Polish immigration to Canada. They left behind famine and flood, occupation and poverty, loved ones and all they knew in Oleszyce and Ruda Różaniecka. Aboard ships christened the SS *Bulgaria* and the SS *Montrose*, they landed in Halifax, Nova Scotia, and Saint John, New Brunswick, and at Ellis Island, New York, eventually homesteading in Manitoba.

On your paternal side, your grandpa Lever fled Columbia, South Carolina, at the age of sixteen. Your grandma Daisy said he left after his brother was beaten to death with a hammer for applying for a white man's job. He journeyed to Chicago, part of the Great Migration of southern African Americans headed north in hopes of a better life. According to Grandma Daisy, your grandfather left Chicago after discovering that the establishment in which he was working as a dishwasher was a front for Al Capone and his illegal enterprises. Fearing for his safety, Grandpa Lever quit working there, and on April 7, 1924, he immigrated to

Canadian Immigration Service*
Form

1. Name: — — **LEVER**     Age: **24**
   (Print name in block letters, family name first)
2. Last permanent address: **422 Calumet Ave, Chicago, Illinois**
3. Sex: **Male**
   Are you married, single, widowed, or divorced: **married**
4. If married are you accompanied by husband or wife? If no give
   name of husband or wife: **No**
5. **Columbia, South Carolina**     Citizenship: **USA**
   (County and P.O.)
6. Object of coming to Canada? **Looking for work**
7. Occupation: **Sleeping Car Porter**
   Will you accept work in Canada? **Yes**
8. Are you able to read? **Yes**  Language: **English**
9. Ever lived in Canada? **No**  Ever refused entry to Canada? **No**
   Race: **Colored**     Religion: **Baptist**
10. Money in possession belonging to passenger: **$129.00**
11. Destined to: **Relative**  Relationship: **Cousin**
12. Name: **Maca Broan (sp)**
13. Address: **181 Maple Street Winnipeg**
    (Passenger must give full address)
14. Are you or any of your family mentally defective? **No**
15. Tuberculosis? **No**  Physically defective? **No**
16. Otherwise debarred under Canadian Immigration? **No**
    Apparent Condition of health? **Good**
17. ACTION TAKEN: **Landed**

*A partial transcription of a Canadian Immigration Service form docu-
menting my grandfather's border crossing through Emerson, Manitoba, on
April 7, 1924.*

Canada and became a porter for the railroad — one of the few
jobs available to Black men at that time.

Your grandpa Mike uprooted Grandma Frances and Aunt
Vee — their "good" daughter, who kept her racial purity — then
hightailed it to the land of the free, home of the brave. In California
there was fresh-squeezed orange juice to go with Grandpa Mike's
vodka, served at "separate but equal" lunch counters.

*J* is for Jezebel.

From the Old Testament, a Phoenician princess.

From Christian lore, a fallen woman.

From the roots of colonialism and the transatlantic slave trade, a racial stereotype.

Black female bodies hypersexualized and made fetish. Daughters, mothers, grandmothers viewed by the white gaze as promiscuous, animalistic, sexualized commodities lacking agency.

*J* is for Jezebel, a symbol positively embraced by me and many other women, a declaration of proudly taking ownership of our bodies, our sexuality and sensuality. No longer accepting the shame, blame, or fetishizing that comes from the white male gaze and patriarchal systems of oppression.

*K* is for KKK.

In 1926 there were chapters of the Ku Klux Klan in Quebec, Ontario, Alberta, and Saskatchewan; the Saskatchewan chapter had over twenty-five thousand members. Memberships cost thirteen dollars. The Klan's presence included acts of domestic terrorism toward Blacks, including cross burnings in Truro, Nova Scotia.

*Truro Daily News*
August 3, 1932, page 1
KKK plan to organize in Truro in early August.
It was understood that a number of klans existed in several towns, including New Glasgow, Stellarton, Halifax; and Saint John and Sackville, New Brunswick.

*Truro Daily News*
August 10, 1932, page 1

The fiery cross of the Ku Klux Klan burned in a fiery manner on Foundry Hill late last night near midnight. The blaze could be seen for miles around while near at hand a couple of hundred or so people watched in silence as the emblem passed into ashes marking the culmination of the first step towards the formation in Truro of a branch of the Invisible Empire Knights of the Ku Klux Klan.

Earlier in the evening a meeting had been held in the Knights of Pythias Hall, Inglis Street, when a prominent Klansman Captain H.E. Walters, Saint John, and Mr. Hoeg, of Saskatchewan, Dominion Organizer, addressed the meeting. There was a large number of people present, estimated at two to three hundred. Organization was proceeded with and the Truro Branch of the Maritime and Newfoundland Division officially organized with fifty or sixty members.

Two years prior in Oakville, Ontario, Klan members kidnapped Ira Johnson, who was Black, in order to prevent his marriage to Isobel Jones, who was white. The day after the incident occurred, Oakville Mayor A.B. Moat made a statement to the press.

*Toronto Daily Star*
March 1, 1930, page 1

"Personally, I think the Ku Klux Klan acted quite properly in the matter. The feeling in the town is generally against such a marriage. Everything was done in an orderly manner. It will be quite an object lesson."

### *L* is for the liturgy in Latin.

*"In nómine Patris, et Fílii, et Spíritus Sancti."*

You loved the ritual as a child, the waft of incense as the censer swayed in the hands of priests. But you couldn't fully embrace a faith that refused to embrace your parents.

Sundays after church service, you'd head to Grandma Daisy and Grandpa Lever's North End home on Cathedral Avenue. They accepted their grandchildren but had difficulty accepting your mother. Troubled waters connected your parents' childhood homes and haunts and working-class neighbourhoods. Your heart would pound as Father's butter-yellow convertible approached the Louise Bridge. You'd hold your breath, cross your fingers, and pray, afraid a hole would materialize as you crossed, that your family's car would plummet into the river and you'd all drown. It was a childhood fear you developed after your aunt and uncle had a serious car accident on a Winnipeg bridge. Until the age of eight, you managed the dread coursing through your body by imagining protective air pockets enveloping the car and transporting all of you safely to the other side.

Once safely at your grandparents', you'd be greeted by Grandma Daisy and the pungent scent of disinfectant. Your grandmother scoured her home with Lysol, a practice which left fumes so potent that your nose stung and your eyes burned and watered as soon as you stepped through the doorway. You considered your grandmother's Lysol use as being the result of trauma; of her being a little girl terrorized by white people who came after the Black enclave in Truro with guns; of her hidden within the hole of an outhouse for safekeeping; of her becoming part of the stink of shit and trauma. The scent of disinfectant lingered on skin, on clothing, on postal-delivered birthday cards, and family history.

Lake Agassiz. Before city, before town, before fort and farmland, colonizer and colonialism, before sweetgrass and bison herds, a glacial lake the size of the Black Sea engulfed what is now called Manitoba, Saskatchewan, and northwestern Ontario.

**$\mathcal{M}$ is for marriage, mother, and matrilineal.**

*Aunt Vee and Uncle Bruno*

*Uncle Leo and Auntie Addie*

*Grandma Frances and Grandpa Mike*

*Mom and Dad*

Your mother shared her womb but not her secrets. No mention of her courtship with your father. No snapshots of the two of them together. No anniversary celebrations. Not a single cherished wedding photograph tucked in a family album.

For a brief time during childhood, you'd ask, "When did you and Daddy get married?" Tight-lipped, your mother would glare in stony silence. Eventually you stopped asking, because you can't get blood from a stone.

Before you were Black,

You were Coloured,

You were mulatto,

You were mixed race,

Caught in a trap not of your choice or creation.

*M* is for mulatto: borrowed from the Spanish and Portugese *mulato*, derived from *mulo* from Latin *mūlus* meaning "mule," the offspring of a horse and donkey.

Mulatto: defined as the first-generation offspring of a Black person and a white person.

Mulatto: as defined by colonialism — Rowan — the offspring of an Africadian/African American father and Polish Canadian mother.

*M* is also for MISSISSIPPI.

A childhood skipping game.

A southern state that repealed its legal ban on miscegenation in 1987.

Mississippi appendectomies: phrase used to describe the non-consensual, medically unnecessary sterilization of Black women in the southern United States.

Mississippi of the North: how your grandma Daisy described her hometown of Truro, Nova Scotia.

**$\mathcal{N}$ is for never.**

"Never get married," your mother said. "Never have children. It'll ruin your life."

**$O$ is for the one-drop rule.**\*

In the United States, the one-drop rule required that any person with a trace of African ancestry be legally classified as Black, regardless of self-identity or attachment to both parents.

Although not officially adopted as law in Canada, the one-drop rule permeates Canada's history.

Fourth Census of Canada 1901
Instructions to Chief Officers, Commissioners
and Enumerators
Section 47. "Only pure whites will be classed as whites; the children begotten of marriages between whites and any one of the other races will be classed as red, black or yellow, as the case may be, irrespective of the degree of colour."

Sixth Census of Canada 1921
Instructions to Commissioners and
Enumerators
Section 94. "The children begotten of marriages between white and black or yellow races will be classified as Negro or Mongolian (Chinese or Japanese), as the case may be."

$O$ is for Octoroon: defined as a person of one-eighth Black ancestry.

Octoroon: your newborn granddaughter, Gracie.

---

\*For additional information, see letters *A, B, C, D, F, G, H, I, K, M, P, Q, R, V, X.*

### *P* is for Polly.

Inferred mother of Rosie, both of whom were born into slavery in South Carolina.

Polly, your inferred great-great-grandmother, who was manumitted by Sebastian Sumter, grandson of General Thomas Sumter, prior to August 6, 1860.

*P* is for passing like ships in the night or between worlds. In historical contexts, *passing* was a way to escape racism. Light-complexioned Black people would cut ties with family, assume a white identity, and move away, never to return.

United States of America, Census Slave Schedule, Sumter County, South Carolina, 1860

National Archives and Records Administration
(NARA microfilm series M653, Roll 1238, Page No. 133)

CENSUS SLAVE SCHEDULE 2
YEAR: 1860
DATE: August 6
STATE: South Carolina
DISTRICT: Sumter
ASSISTANT MARSHALL: ?

| PG# | LN# | NAME OF SLAVE-OWNER | #OF SLAVES | AGE | SEX | COLOR | FUGITIVE FROM STATE | MANU-MITTED |
|---|---|---|---|---|---|---|---|---|
| 133. | 1. | Sebastian Sumter. | | | | | | |
| 133. | 17. | | 26* | 5 | F. | B. | | |
| 133. | 25. | | 34** | 32 | F. | B. | | X |

*Rosie-inferred
**Polly-inferred

You dreamed of having daughters, of having blue-eyed, blond-haired babies. For a time, you felt the only way you could protect your children from racism was to hope they'd physically resemble you as little as possible.

*P* is for Persephone, who was kidnapped by Hades to become his bride in the underworld. When allowed to return to her grief-stricken mother, Persephone was still bound to Hades because she had eaten seeds from the pomegranate while in the underworld. Every seed she had consumed obligated Persephone to live one month of each year with Hades in the land of the dead.

*P* is for pregnancy.

Beth: You became pregnant by your high school boyfriend, R. Not knowing where to turn, you went to a pregnancy distress service, which arranged prenatal care. When you were about seven months along, your belly swollen, your doctor asked, "What do you plan on doing with the baby?" Shocked, you asked him what he meant. "Well," he said, "there are so many childless couples who would just love to adopt a newborn." Shaking, you told him you were keeping your baby.

Raven: You met your father at the Bay's Paddlewheel restaurant. Against the backdrop of a faux-Mississippi riverboat, and with Beth beside you in a high chair, you said to your father, "Guess what? I'm expecting." He frowned. Shook his head. Said, "You should have an abortion. You don't want to wind up some fat slob pumping out babies on welfare."

Annabella: It took years to have Annabella — your final baby, your final C-section, one of three incision scars you consider a badge of honour.

*P* is for premonitions: You come from a line of women who believed in superstitions and premonitions — information you didn't share with Sarah, the hospital chaplin, as you sat in a private room assigned for family. Down the hall, your newborn, premature granddaughter Gracie was in the neonatal intensive care unit. A floor above, your daughter Beth was in the maternal intensive care unit after the delivery, fighting for her life. You considered telling Sarah that a few weeks before you had had a premonition, an image flash of Beth in an operating room, lying beneath bloody sheets, on a bloody table, the floor coated with your daughter's blood. But you didn't tell her. Just as you didn't tell Beth. Even though you'd had premonitions that had come true in the past, you remained silent. You didn't want to add to the stress of a high-risk pregnancy by being a drama queen.

### *Q* is for queen.

A gentle snowfall. A queen sat next to an open window, embroidering on an ebony frame. She pricked her finger and three drops of blood fell onto the snow. "Oh, that I had a child as white as snow, as red as blood, and as black as the wood of the embroidery frame," the queen said. It wasn't long until she had a daughter, with skin as white as snow, lips as red as blood, and hair as black as ebony.

Quadroon: defined as a person of one-quarter Black ancestry.

Quadroon: your daughters, Beth, Raven, and Annabella.

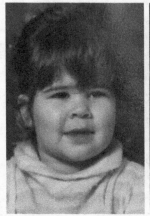  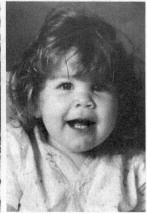

*Beth*          *Raven*          *Annabella*

Welfare queen: a derogatory stereotype. A label marginalizing and morally judging women living in poverty. A racist narrative depicting Black women as lazy, unmotivated, and sexually promiscuous, having baby after baby after baby in order to collect welfare cheques.

Welfare queen: a racist trope your father seemed to accept without question, and one that you did your best to dissociate from by getting your university education while raising babies and also working part-time.

◆

### ℛ is for race.

> Race is the child of racism, not the father.
>
> — Ta-Nehisi Coates

*R* is for red welts and open wounds. Crimson splotches on walls and floors. Your grandma Daisy beat her children, made them scrub away bloodstains on hands and knees. She carried a torch, a tortured soul, the overseer's lash handed down like a baton through generations.

*R* is for roots firmly planted, damaged, lost, or stolen.

*Roots*: a Pulitzer Prize–winning novel by Alex Haley. A televised miniseries which premiered January 23, 1977. It told the generational saga of an African American family and starred LeVar Burton as the enslaved African Kunta Kinte.

*Roots*: a movie that was hard for you to watch, reminding you of a home you could never return to, a language lost to your tongue, loved ones missing, loved ones you would never know.

*R* is for *Rosa*: Latin for "rose."

Rose: a girl's name. A flower and symbol of love, believed to have magical properties to ward off vampires.

The most common and inexpensive way to cultivate roses is by grafting, the joining of one rose variety with the hardier rootstock of another cultivar. A downside to propagation in this manner? Rootstocks have a tendency to sucker and to revert to their natural state.

"You make sure people know you're Black," your mother said,

whenever someone would mistake you for white, for Spanish, Filipina, East Asian, First Nations, Tahitian, Hawaiian.

A rose, a grandmother, by any other name? Rosie S., Rosie K., Rosalia G., Rozalia Z., and Rozalia W.

Ruda Różaniecka: the tiny village in Poland where your maternal ancestors came from. *Ruda*: Polish (fem), meaning "ore." *Różaniecka*: Polish (fem), from *różaniec*, meaning "rosary." The rosary: beads used by Catholics during prayer.

Rowan: borrowed from early Scandinavian, meaning "rowan tree." Also, Gaelic, meaning "red." Rowan, another name for mountain ash. Genus: *Sorbus*. Family: Rosaceae. A tree with reddish berries that grew from wild seed in your garden. In parts of Europe, the rowan tree is believed to have protective and magical powers; is a favoured wood for fashioning dousing rods, also crosses and stakes to ward off evil spirits and vampires.

Rowan: a name you legally adopted years ago, having no idea the connections you'd later make.

*S* **is for soap opera.**

Q. If your family had a soap opera, what would it be called?
A. *Black and Blues*.

*S* is for *sub rosa*: Latin for "secret." Secret pasts. Secret pacts. Secret crush. Family secrets. Open secrets. Best-kept secrets, like the ones kept by Canada, a country in which slavery was practised for over two hundred years.

*Nova Scotia Gazette and Weekly Chronicle*
May 30, 1752, page 2
(Nova Scotia Archives microfilm number 8152)
Just imported and to be sold by Joshua Mauger,
at Major Lockman's Store in Halifax several
Negro Slaves, viz. A very likely Negro Wench,

of about thirty five Years of Age, a Creole born,
has been brought up in a Gentleman's Family,
and capable of doing all sorts of Work belonging
thereto, as Needle-Work of all sorts, and in the
best Manner; also Washing, Ironing, Cookery,
and every other Thing that can be expected from
such a Slave.

Stigma. Stigmata: the manifestations of lesions having divine origins, which echo the bleeding wounds found on Christ's crucified body. Stigmata, from the Greek *stigma*, meaning "tattoo," a brand mark of ownership made on the body of an animal or slave. How many of us carry the scars, the self-inflicted wounds for sins not our own?

A year after your mother died, your maternal cousin Michael told you he'd known since childhood that your parents had to get married. The scarlet letter *M*, for mistake, was no longer yours to bear.

🝆

### *T* is for time.

Does time heal all wounds?

*T* is for tree, as in apple, as in crab, as in the tree of knowledge, of good and of evil. Trees provide shade, shelter, and sustenance. Trees provide branches for hanging swings and runaway slaves.

*T* is for Thursday's child, who had oh so far to go.

*Nova Scotia Gazette and Weekly Chronicle*
September 1, 1772, page 2
(Nova Scotia Archives microfilm number 8152)
Ran away from her Master JOHN ROCK, on
Monday the 18th Day of August last; a Negroe

Girl named *Thursday*, about four and an half feet high, broad sett [*sic*], with a Lump above her Right Eye; Had on when she run away a red Cloth Petticoat, a red Baize Bed Gown, and a red Ribbon about her Head. Whosoever may harbour said Negroe Girl, or encourage her to stay away from her said Master, may depend on being prosecuted according as the Law shall direct. And whosoever may be so kind to take her up and send her home to her said Master, shall be paid all Costs and Charges, together with TWO DOLLARS Reward for their Trouble.

JOHN ROCK, HALIFAX, Sept, 1772.

*T* is for texts and the Trans-Canada Highway.

It was 1,371 kilometres from Winnipeg to Calgary. By the time you reached the Petro-Canada station in Brandon, the texts started coming from Jason, Beth's husband, in Calgary.

*T* is for time stamps.

**11:55 AM**

**Jason:**

Please pray, rushing to hospital from ultrasound. Baby's heartbeat has been low then high. We could be delivering today.

**Rowan:**

Please take care. I'm sending prayers. Keep me posted!!!!!!!!!! I thought I'd be there on time. Send Beth my love and tell her Mama's on her way.

*T* is for trepidation.

**12:15 PM**

They say it's over 50% chance the baby's coming today.
Just confirmed. It's happening today.

Did you get my text? We're at the hospital now.
This baby might be coming now.

*T* is for the time that it took to safely pull your car off the highway.

**12:17 PM**

Baby is coming and Beth is in the
operating room now. Please pray.

I just saw your texts. I was on the highway. Please
send her my love and blessings for Beth and baby.
I hate that I'm not there!!!

Baby's here.

How's Beth? How's baby? How are you?

Baby's great. Such a cutie. Will send
pic shortly. Can you let her sisters know?

*T* is for "Tell me that my daughter is okay."

**12:27 PM**

How's baby? When will Beth be out of surgery?
Were you able to be with her?

She's still in the operating room. Lost lots of blood cuz of fibroids but they're taking care of her.

*T* is for transfusions of life-saving blood.

**12:30 PM**

Congrats papa. I'll text the girls. What'd baby weigh?

Four pounds, I think. 😊

Congrats. Sending you guys so much love. I'll be there as soon as possible. Keep me posted.

Thanks. Will send photo once Beth's awake.
I want her to see the little one before everyone else!

My girl's superwoman!!!!! Can't wait to see pics and meet baby in person. 💜 She's a miracle.

*T* is for thankful.

**1:34 PM**

Beth's finally stabilized and is going to be moved to ICU shortly. Things are much better now. Still not fully out of the woods but this is appreciated news.

Thank you, universe. Almost at Regina.

Now, she needs to start healing.

Yes, healing and rest. She has mommy duty for the next forever. 💜

First positive news of the day besides the birth.
They're not needing blood anymore, praise God!
She's not out of the woods, but they're not rushing in
and out anymore asking for more blood.

> You tell her Mama is on the way. I absolutely hate
> not being there. I feel sick. All I want is for my baby
> to be okay. Driving into Regina.

## *T* is for turn of events.

### 2:46 PM

Just got an update. They have to do a hysterectomy.
She's losing too much blood and they want to keep her
alive and so do I. Please send up prayers.

> How is she doing? I just pulled off
> the highway to check texts. How are
> things going Jason?

## *T* is for terrified.

### 3:10 PM

No idea. They're trying to stop the bleeding and are
giving her transfusions. She's fighting but they say it's
touch and go. So, we need prayers for the bleeding to
stop. My dad's here with me right now. Just wanted to
give you an update.

> Please have them take care of her Jason.
> I know they are. I'm just freaked out
> because I'm not there.

Drive safe please! They are doing all they can
and Beth's a fighter!

She's not at the ICU yet. They're back in surgery to work
on her again. She needs to start clotting. Know better in
the next couple hours.

Tell her Mama is on her way. I hate not being there.
I feel sick. All I want is for my baby to be okay. I'll text
from Swift Current. Tell her I love her and
she's strong. So strong.

*T* is for thoughts and prayers uttered out loud and offered in silence from behind the steering wheel. *T* is for telepathic connection, the ability to transmit to your daughter the strength to survive.

**6:59 PM**

Doctor came to see us and said she's slowly getting better.
Thanks for your support and prayers throughout the day.

What hospital is she at? I'm driving straight
through to Calgary.

Foothills. I'm going to see her now. If you're tired, stay
safe and rest. It's not a fun drive to do all at once. Will
keep you updated.

She's semi awake. That's a good sign.
Tell her I love her and I'm coming!!!!!

Thank goodness. I'll see you guys as soon as I
can. So thankful things have turned a corner. I was
soooooooooooo freaking out!!!!!!!!!!!!!! Sending hugs to all.

Drive safe, first and foremost. Love ya. She's in good
hands! They're doing miracles. It wasn't a normal day for
the Unit or the doctors. I can't imagine the roller coaster
of emotion driving and hearing all the updates. Beth's
doing really well and been stable for four hours. Take
breaks. You don't need to get here ASAP, but I'm not
gonna stop you. She's your baby! 😊

I'll drive extra careful when it gets dark but I'll be there.

*T* is for transfusions; the three times Beth had her body's total
blood volume replaced. *T* is also for thanks. Your gratitude for the
sixty people who had previously donated blood products — without their generous gifts, your daughter would have died.

**𝒰 is for uterus, uteri; also, for uterine fibroids.**

Benign growths that range in size from microscopic seeds to peas,
to fists, to cantaloupes, to pumpkins. Black women are three times
more likely than the rest of the female population to develop them,
and have five times higher odds of harsher symptoms.

Sistas, raised since slave days to be strong and carry on, suffer in silence — the heavier bleeding, the anemia, the excruci-
ating pelvic pain. Earlier onset of uterine fibroids can lead to
infertility, high-risk pregnancy, and miscarriage; to the increased
likelihood of delivery by Caesarean section and of life-altering
hysterectomies.

Two of your three daughters have severe uterine fibroids. At
times, you've felt guilty. Had you somehow cursed them with your
genetics? Had historical traumas taken hold and expressed themselves on a cellular level? Had you passed on, biologically, the traumatic memories of mothers, of Mother Africa, of Middle Passage,
like you had the wayward kinks and red undertones of your hair?

*V* is for vampire.

You mistakenly thought vampires wore black capes and Victorian garb and only came out at night. In reality, vampires are not afraid of daylight. They're afraid of the truth being told, of being seen, of being glimpsed behind their public masks. They wear polyester and silk, checkered shirts and skirts over checkered pasts, coats with London Fog labels, pressed jeans and worn wool cardigans over pit-stained dress shirts — hiding in plain sight under the guise of goodness, of parent, of friend, of lover.

*V* is for voices; those messages that became imprinted on your psyche over the years.

Mother: *Nobody loves you. If you think someone does, you're either kidding yourself, too stupid to know better, or both. The world will screw you just as soon as look at you. You think you're so special with your nose in that book. You're too fat, too thin, too much. You ruined my life. You're the only one who can convince your father not to leave us for that woman. You're a user just like your father.*

Father: *As the matriarch of the family it's your job to pay the bills, raise the kids, keep house, and please your man. I know a woman who started working out at the gym not long after her C-section. You'll ruin your life if you have that baby. Be the best of the best. Appearance is all that matters. I'm heading out. I won't be long. I'm staying just for you.*

One side of the family said: *Take care of your mother so she doesn't wind up killing herself.*

The other side said: *Take care of your father. Look how hard his life is being a Black man, married to your mother.*

Both sides believed loyalty was all that mattered, that blood was thicker than water, but blood tithes flowed only one way.

Men: *You're so exotic. You're quite the lover. Quite the tease. Such a liar. I gave up everything for you. You're the one who invited me in. You ruined my life.*

Society: *What are you? Where are your people from? You're too white, too black. You don't belong.*

*V* is for Viola Desmond, "Canada's Rosa Parks," who refused to give up her seat and be relocated to the balcony section, referred to as "nigger heaven," at the Roseland Theatre in Nova Scotia.

*V* is for vestige. You search your newborn granddaughter's face, hoping to see some vestige of yourself, no longer thinking you're selfish for doing so.

### *W* is for water.

We are made and come from water. We begin life, tiny embryos with slit-like structures resembling gills.

*Wagobagitik*: the Mi'kmaq name for the Truro region, meaning "end of the water's flow."

You carry womb-like remembrances of water. Born on the prairie, a sea of rustling wheat stalks, you're drawn to the forks of the Red and Assiniboine Rivers, to the white sand beaches of Lake Winnipeg, to ocean shores and salt-water breezes where your body relaxes and your hair happily curls from the humidity.

### XX. XY.

Why? You have no idea what drew your parents together.

Did the blood of Malcolm X mark the spot where your parents danced under stars, even then bearing the scars of family history, the legacies of slavery and Jim Crow, old-country poverty, wounds carried like excess baggage into their brave new world?

*Y* **is for yellow strands of embroidery thread wrapped around your wrist.**

They are reminders of your daughter Beth and your newborn granddaughter, Gracie. You gathered in celebration to honour Beth's entry into motherhood as friends, as family, as mothers, daughters, and grandmothers. Once your daughter was home, after weeks in the hospital, you broke bread, shared wine and stories, and made solemn vows that everyone would be Beth and Gracie's village, there to support, to guide, to love, and to nurture.

*Z* **is for Zion Baptist Church, established 1896, in Truro, Nova Scotia.**

*Z*, a letter of the alphabet pronounced "zed" and sometimes "zee." *Z*, an unknown quantity in algebraic equations; a girl unknown to her family and community, and called "zebra" on the playground. A girl who, in the end, chose not Black or white, not either or, not one or the other, but chose her self entirely.

**Binding Resolutions**

The following contract **(1)** has been reached between _____ (historically known of as the expert, dear friend, the expert, soulmate, the expert, her knight in shining armour, the expert, the giver of rules and remonstrations and hereafter to be referred to as the "First Party") and _____ (historically known as dear friend, hero **(2)**, human — no longer Martian **(3)**, his favourite person, secret-keeper, soulmate, Tahiti Sweetie, Babe, Hon, favourite storyteller, teller of tall tales, crier of Lucille Ball–worthy tears, the love of his life, his biggest mistake, and hereafter referred to as the "Second Party") (collectively, to be known as the "Parties").

(1) A binding agreement previously unwritten, with parts unspoken. Any and all damages to the Second Party's self-esteem, sense of safety and security, hope for the present and future, or her emotional, psychological, physical, financial, or spiritual well-being will be the ~~soul~~ sole responsibility of the Second Party. In no way, and at no time, will the First Party consider himself accountable for any harm done.

(2) While the Second Party does not believe in the idolization and creation of heroes, the First Party insists upon putting the Second Party onto a precarious pedestal. It should also be noted that the First Party expects to be celebrated and recognized as the Second Party's knight in shining armour, who rescued her from an abusive marriage and her gothically fucked-up family of origin.

(3) The Martian analogy carries

The parties are about to enter a long-term relationship **(4)**, including marriage **(5)**.

This Agreement establishes the respective rights **(6)**, responsibilities **(7)**, and obligations under the relationship, upon marriage, and upon the possibility of a separation or dissolution of the marriage.

**1. Rules:** see **(6)** and **(8)**.

**2. Obligations**

The First Party states that since he has freely and without reservation given of the following to the Second Party: his heart, soul, body, love, hopes and dreams for the future, career, and personal reputation, that the Second Party is therefore bound in perpetuity to the following rules **(8)**:

a. No matter what, the Parties are to have ongoing, deep-diving conversations on any and all subjects the First Party finds of interest.

b. The Second Party will demonstrate undying adoration.

c. The Second Party is never to lie to the First Party.

d. The Second Party is never to leave the First Party.

e. And under pain of death, she is not supposed to tell.

deep meaning to the Second Party, ever since reading *The Martian Chronicles* by Ray Bradbury during her adolescence. The Martian characterized her perception of being a function, shapeshifting into whatever form/fantasy was demanded of her.

(4) Despite evidence to the contrary, the First Party will vigorously defend his characterization of this being a loving, caring, and healthy relationship between two consenting adults.

(5) Two days before Halloween, with marriage licence in tow, the Parties will walk up the concrete steps to the City Courthouse. The Second Party will notice a trio of office workers dressed in costumes, especially the figure wearing fangs, a Black cape with red lining. Historically, she has been a real sucker for vampires.

His mother and brother will be the only witnesses in attendance. Despite wanting her daughters and best friend with her, no one will be told about the wedding until days, weeks after he's put a ring on it.

(6) Please note: The Second Party will have no rights. None.

(7) As a courtesy, the First Party will provide constant reminders that she bears all responsibility for the formation of this relationship. His words will become seared into her neural pathways, become a statement of blame echoing

in her mind for years after she leaves him. *You were the one who asked for a kiss. You were the one who invited me in. You were the one who asked for a kiss. You were the one who invited me in. You were the one who asked for a kiss. You were the one who invited me in.*

(8) Although the rules will be problematic to the Second Party during the entire span of the relationship, they will prove especially daunting during the formulation of a safety plan with Donna, her domestic-abuse support worker. Regardless, the First Party nevertheless strenuously insists that the rules be adhered to.

The Second Party will feel deep shame, guilt, and immeasurable terror as she meets with Donna in her tiny office with a window overlooking a busy street, with the view she will never notice because of the need to sit facing the door in case she feels the pressing desire to bolt.

Despite stating that abandonment is her issue, the words *until death do you part* will take on a whole new meaning.

The Second Party will take seriously the First Party's claims that if anyone crossed him, he wouldn't be suicidal, he would be homicidal; that he is an expert shot and received the highest scores in marksmanship while attending the police academy; that he has past acquaintances who would be more than willing to do physical harm to anyone who crossed him.

**2. Obligations cont'd (9)** It is the duty of the Second Party to fulfill the below-listed obligations in a consistent and cheerful manner, with no semblance of hanky-panky except under the circumstances of sexual role play at the request and behest of the First Party:

a. Expressing eternal gratitude.

b. Playing the role of blissful, domestic housewife.

c. Fulfilling any and all sexual fantasies.

d. Silencing her voice.

e. Ignoring her perceptions.

f. Accepting without protest his right **(10)** to discount her perceptions by the methods of gaslighting, victim blaming, guilting, mind-fucking, exercising intimidation, and/or any other technique the First Party discovers that proves useful.

### 3. Responsibilities

The First Party believes that the following are the gender-specific responsibilities owed to a wife upon marriage:

The 3 P's of Domesticity **(11)**

a. Provide

b. Procreate

c. Protect

### 4. Domicile (12)

After the First Party abandons his wife and marriage, but before cohabitation

(9) As an admirer of the 1960s traditional household, the First Party states that he always wanted to play Dick Van Dyke in the suburbs. Although the Second Party is a fan of midcentury modern design, and of wearing black capris and hairbands, ballet flats, and the occasional starched white cotton shirt, she never intended to become a Stepford wife.

(10) Please refer back to note (6) for further explanation.

(11)

a. The First Party will hold the Second Party responsible for any and all disruption to his employment and income.

b. The First Party, claiming to be sterile, sees no need for birth control. When the Second Party becomes pregnant, he will coax, cajole, and coerce her into having an abortion, which he will pay for. Having been isolated, she will have no one to confide in. The procedure will cost $500 and he will accompany her to the clinic. The Second Party will never forgive herself for not being able to stand up to him and protect Dylan, the name she gives to the baby she will never hold in her arms.

c. The First Party categorically denies being abusive.

(12) If home is where the heart is, she will wonder, where do the broken-hearted reside?

with the Second Party, he will move into a high-rise apartment building located next to the Red River. From the balcony of his one-bedroom apartment are views of the Second Party's suburban neighbourhood and her favourite park from childhood. He will state that his ex-wife finds it interesting how convenient the location is to the Second Party. **(13)**

The Second Party resides in a three-bedroom bungalow purchased prior to meeting the First Party, located in a suburb with streets given botanical names.

She will have vigorously fought to keep her home after leaving her abusive marriage to H. She will have transformed the front yard into a cottage garden as a way to deal with her grief, her loss, and the shame. **(14)**

On Wednesday evenings the First Party will drive the Second Party to his apartment where the two of you will drink wine and fuck. **(15)**

In two years, he will move into her home, which she shares with her daughters.

The Parties therefore agree to as follows:

## 5. Period of Cohabitation

Cohabitation: a state of living together and having a sexual relationship prior to

(13) It will be a fifteen-minute car ride across the Chief Peguis Bridge to the home owned by the Second Party.

(14) The following perennials, shrubs, and trees were planted by the Second Party:
a. Amur Maple – 2
b. Crimson Frost Birch – 2
c. Japanese Tree Lilac – 1
d. Dropmore Honeysuckle – 1
e. Red Osier Dogwood – 5
f. Brandon Pyramidal Cedar – 10
g. Autumn Joy Sedum – 5
h. Sedum groundcover
i. Adelaide Hoodless Rose – 3
j. Georgie's Peony – 1
k. Daylily – 13
l. Wild Rose – 6
m. Yarrow – 9
n. Baby's Breath – 3
o. Cranesbill Geranium – 5
p. Queen Anne's Lace – 10
q. Purple Coneflower – 7
r. Shasta Daisy – 5
s. Rudbeckia – 3
t. Blue Fescue – 5
u. Variegated Karl Foerster Feather Reed Grass – 7
v. Prairie Traveller's Joy Clematis – 5
w. Virginia Creeper – 8
x. Stella D'Oro Daylily – 7
y. Datura, Angel's Trumpet – 3
z. Mountain Ash – 1

(15) He will attribute the Second Party's panic attacks to having been sexually abused in childhood.

marriage, the state or fact of living or existing in the same time and place. **(16)**

It is the position of the First Party that the two Parties, being soulmates, have known each other through various lifetimes and that this most recent manifestation is just the latest incarnation of their existence of being together.

It must be noted that in the event the Second Party leaves the "marriage," the period of cohabitation will continue nonetheless. The First Party will become a permanent lodger in the Second Party's mind, taking up valuable emotional real estate, giving ongoing and constant feedback loops of what a fuckup the Second Party is and how the First Party gave up everything for her. **(17)**

## 6. Ownership and Division of Property

### a. Assets and ~~Lie~~ Li abilities

The First Party represents that Schedule A contains a complete and accurate disclosure of all assets and liabilities registered in his name and of which he is the beneficial owner.

The Second Party represents that Schedule A contains a complete and accurate disclosure of all assets and liabilities registered in her name and of which she is the beneficial owner.

(16) He will move in August and the Parties will be married in October, two days before her youngest daughter celebrates her seventh Halloween.

(17) The Second Party will believe that she will never be free of him. All she has done is moved the cage. There will be no letting go of the relationship, unless the First Party decides otherwise.

This Agreement is signed on the date indicated below.

FIRST PARTY

_____ *(signature)*
Name:
Date:

WITNESS 1*

_____ *(signature)*
Name:
Date:

SECOND PARTY

_____ *(signature)*
Name:
Date:

WITNESS 2*

_____ *(signature)*
Name:
Date:

* Please note that, although this Agreement offers provision of Witnesses to the above contract, given the First Party's demand for secrecy, no witnesses will be party to the signing of this agreement. Nor is the signature of the Second Party required to provide consent.

** The Second Party must understand that the First Party will make continuous remarks about his preparing to leave her if she doesn't fall into line. It will take years for her to understand that this was an empty threat meant to manipulate her into compliance.

*(Cont.)*

\*\*\* The First Party will state:

- *I'm only telling you these things because I love you. So that when I leave it won't come as a surprise.*
- *I don't want to leave. I'm giving you a warning so you can change what you're doing.*

\*\*\*\* The First Party will also state:

- *I don't want this (meaning a threatened divorce) to cost a lot.*
- *I want to leave in the best shape possible.*
- *I don't see the need for lawyers.*
- *I'm a reasonable guy, for the most part.*

## Articulations of Loss

## ACROSS

2. Constellations of consonants illuminating dim paths to nowhere.

4. Barbed tongue. Barbed wire. Trip.

5. A shotgun splatter of hit and miss articulations.

6. Twenty-eight days of politic remembrances.

7. Mother, was it shame that held your tongue or something else?

8. What are you? What are you? What are you?

9. Self-love spoken in a language of erasure.

14. What is home but an unknown quantity?

15. *Babcie moje, zawołałabym Was ale słowa zamierają mi na języku.*

16. Hidden variables of heartache.

## DOWN

1. Equations of irreparable loss.

3. My tongue stumbles over eurocolonial fault lines.

4. Silence does not become you.

10. I wander barren shorelines, collecting lost worlds inside the dark whorl of mollusk shells. One day, I will hear you whisper home.

11. My foreign accent betrays me.

12. Suspect appearances. No, really. Where are you from?

13. A homeland lost in translation.

17. The palm of my hand holds echolocations of causalities. Links broken across time and ocean tides.

Trialogue: A Play On Words

CAST: in order of appearance

| | |
|---|---|
| ROWAN | Rowan McCandless |
| M | M |
| THE DIRECTOR | Himself |
| THE WRITER | Herself |
| SARA, Rowan's best friend | Sara |
| THE POLICE DETECTIVE | M |
| THE NEIGHBOUR | Rowan McCandless |
| THE SCIENTIST | Rowan McCandless |
| THE MATHEMATICIAN | M |
| THE UNSUSPECTING VICTIM | Rowan McCandless |
| THE MYSTERIOUS STRANGER | M |
| THE GIRLFRIENDS 1. 2. | Uncredited |
| THE WAITER | Uncredited |

TRIALOGUE: A PLAY ON WORDS

**SCENE ONE**
**FADE IN.**
**INT. MIDCENTURY MODERN HOME/PRINCIPAL BEDROOM – DAY**
There is a queen-sized bed with a simple antique metal bedframe. Atop the mattress is a Marimekko duvet set and coordinating pillows. On each side of the bed are matching wooden dressers. Alongside one wall is a series of ladder bookcases filled with books and a few orange-coloured knick-knacks. On the wall opposite to the numerous books lining the shelves is a white-painted dresser and a mirror with a white wooden frame. Across from the bed is a large closet, from which hangs both men's and women's clothing.

Inside this "perfect" suburban home is **ROWAN**. She is wearing a grey sweatshirt and black leggings. Her hair is held in a sloppy bun. She is curled up beneath a nubby throw blanket on what appears to be her side of the bed.

At the sound of footsteps in the hallway, her body stiffens, and she pulls the blanket over her head.

**M** enters the room. He is wearing a checkered shirt and blue jeans. He appears to be annoyed.

> M
> Rowan. Are you awake?

Rowan takes a deep breath and sighs. She pulls the blanket away from her face.

> ROWAN
> I was just trying to take a nap.

> M
> You're always trying to take a nap. Either that or you're writing or watching Netflix on your cellphone with your earbuds crammed in your ears. I feel like you're avoiding me, and I don't like being treated this way.

M stands closer to ROWAN's side of the bed.

ROWAN sits up and nervously plays with the fringes of the throw blanket.

> M
> You know, we hád dreams once upon a time, and now we don't talk, we don't touch, and that pretty much violates everything that we were about. I've tried to communicate this to you, both verbally and in writing, and all I'm left with is feeling unheard, unloved, and unappreciated. I started out so keen … like you've been so cold over the last long while. It seems to me that you called this

thing off a long time ago but just haven't put it into words. I'm figuring I lost you long before New York City and I don't know what it was.

ROWAN begins to cry.

                    M
And then you're throwing that shit at me, telling me I'm *that* guy. That guy who would betray things you told me in confidence to your daughters. I meet that with a fair amount of disdain, you know. You have no idea who I am. I'm some living embodiment of some character actor you've created. I wouldn't be here if I was that guy.

                  ROWAN
We can't begin to learn how to talk to one another by ourselves. We can't begin to figure things out by ourselves.

                    M
So, you're saying it's either couples therapy or it's over, is that right? Is that right? Come on, Rowan, just answer the fucking question!

                    ROWAN
Other people go to see a couples
therapist, and it's not some aw-
ful, terrible thing to do.


                      M
As if you have any faith in therapy.

ROWAN stops crying and sits up in bed.

                    ROWAN
Don't put that on me. I've been
in the eating disorders program
and I'm seeing one of their therapists. I'm working on my stuff.


                      M
For all the fat lot of good it's
doing for you. Look, I'm angry
and upset that you think it's impossible for me to understand
you without having a third party
present.


                    ROWAN
That's not what I said. What I said
was that it is impossible for me
to understand you without a third
party present. I'm saying that it's
impossible for me to understand
our *relationship* without —

                    M

A third party present. A third
party present. I don't know if
you're obtuse or if something else
is going on, because you know what
will happen if we go. We either lie
and make a farce of couples therapy or I realize that we should
get a divorce, which means we just
spent a shit ton of money we don't
have in the process. Or we tell
the truth and jeopardize my career. And I don't understand why
you just don't get it … You know
what we could do is go back to
what we used to do. Having weekly
meetings to discuss what's going
on in our relationship … Look, you
don't have to answer right now,
just think about it and get back
to me.


M walks toward the doorway. He pauses at the
threshold.


                    M

Out of curiosity, are you ever going to get back to me about the
note I wrote you?


                 ROWAN

There's no point. I know the rules
well enough. I'm not supposed to

> say anything about our relation-
> ship, so there's nothing for me to
> write.

M smiles in satisfaction and nods before leaving
the room.

ROWAN pulls M's note from under her pillow.
CLOSE-UP SHOT: The note M has written and given
to her.

**TRIALOGUE: A PLAY ON WORDS**
**Act One**
**Therapist: So, what brought you here?**
**Husband: My wife tells me that she can't talk to me
unless a third party is in the room.**
**Wife: I think it's the only thing we can do to change what's
happening.**
**Therapist: What's happening?**
**Wife: Our marriage is falling apart. I can't fix it. I want
somebody to fix it.**

ROWAN (V.O.)

Hold on a minute. I really don't think I would
say that. I hate it when he presumes to know
what I'm thinking or feeling.

DIRECTOR

Cut. Look, just stick to the script.

ROWAN

That's all I've been doing in this relationship,
sticking to the script.

DIRECTOR

The script is the script.

M

Exactly, that's what I've been telling her all along.

ROWAN

Fine. Have it your way.

M

I always do.

DIRECTOR

Can we pick up from the therapist, "What's happening?" And action.

CLOSE-UP of M's note continues.

**Therapist: What's happening?**
**Wife: Our marriage is falling apart. I can't fix it. I want somebody to fix it.**
**Husband: I can't fix it. Believe me, I've tried. I am giving up.**
**Wife: It's like he's blaming me — he's saying it's my fault. He's the professional, the expert.**
**Husband: Yeah ... it was a lot of work to find someone in the business who didn't know or hadn't heard of me. But then we came upon you.**
**Wife: So, you can fix this, right?**
**Therapist: What is this?**
**Wife: Silence. Distance. Disapproval. Conflict when we bump into one another.**
**Husband: Yup.**

**Therapist: Okay, let me start. How did you guys meet? What drew you together? (Now, Rowan, you write Act Two.)**

                        ROWAN (V.O.)
This note is such B.S.

On the other side of the soundstage is a grouping of chairs for the director and actors. Industrial lighting hangs from metal beams on the ceiling. The floor is polished concrete. Cameras and mike booms overwhelm the setting.

    The DIRECTOR, annoyed, jumps from his chair.

                        DIRECTOR
    Cut!

M is sitting in his chair, smoking a cigarette and drinking a dirty vodka martini.

                        M
    Don't encourage her.

ROWAN pulls down the sleeves of her sweatshirt.

                        ROWAN
                      (mumbles)
    Sometimes, I wish that you would just shut the
    fuck up.

                        WRITER
                      (nervous)
    We can try another script. I know, what if
    this was a romantic comedy, a boy-meets-girl,

boy-loses-girl, boy-gets-girl-back scenario, then perhaps the two characters could meet at a coffee shop.

ROWAN

But I don't even drink coffee.

DIRECTOR

It's called acting, dear, for a reason. People, take your places.

SCENE TWO
FADE IN.
INT. ARTISANAL CAFÉ/A TABLE NEXT TO THE WINDOW
— DAY
The café is busy. The baristas are doing their best to keep up with the demands of patrons, mostly office workers, on their lunch break. ROWAN, wearing jeans and an orange sweater, is nursing a chai latte as she sits at a table next to an oversized picture window. Across from ROWAN is SARA, her estranged best friend since high school, who is similarly dressed in jeans and a sweater. SARA adds sugar to her cup of coffee.

ROWAN

Hold on. Why are we bringing Sara into this?

DIRECTOR

Cut!

ROWAN

Can't we leave Sara out of this?

WRITER
(speaks through gritted teeth)
She's the one who introduced you to M. I'm just
aiming for a bit of authenticity. Come on, work
with me here.

ROWAN
But we haven't seen one another in years. Sara,
I hope this isn't too awkward for you, especially
after … you know.

SARA
It's all right. I had the sense you didn't exactly
write that letter cutting me off on your own. I
know M had his hands all over it. But just to be
clear, and I'm not trying to hurt you here, this
isn't the start of renewing our friendship. I've
moved on and don't want to re-establish contact.
I say this without malice, and I do wish you well,
I really do, but there's no way to pick up from
where things were left all those years ago.

DIRECTOR
All right, people, enough with the chit-chat.
Everyone take your places … and action!

ROWAN sits across from her best friend, SARA, at
a table set next to an oversized picture window.
In the background is the smooth mix of clas-
sic jazz, the sound of milk being frothed, the
hiss of a Mastrena high-performance espresso
machine. The two are in the midst of conversation as M walks into the cafe, carrying a blue

backpack. SARA notices him and waves him over. M waves back. He gestures *just a minute* before standing in line to place his coffee order.

> ROWAN
>
> I take it you know the guy.

SARA nods.

> SARA
>
> For quite some time now. I met him at university. He was one of my in-structors. He's a really great guy. More like an honorary woman … you know, really sensitive and perfect-ly safe.

M walks toward their table carrying a cup of coffee.

After introductions, and much conversation, SARA leaves to catch a bus home. ROWAN and M remain, chatting.

> ROWAN
>
> And so that's what I'm trying to figure out, how best to help my daughter with her grief issues.

> M
>
> Having two close friends pass away within a few months is tough at any age, but especially at fifteen.

ROWAN tears up.

> ROWAN
>
> I just want to give her the sup-
> port she needs to get through this
> and be okay. Sorry, I didn't mean
> to get all emotional. Ugh.

> M
>
> There's no apology necessary. It's
> a good thing to feel your emo-
> tions … You know, I'm thinking
> that if you want to be helpful to
> your daughter, maybe you should
> see a therapist to deal with your
> grief issues.

> ROWAN
>
> I don't think that I have any grief
> issues.

> M
>
> But didn't you tell me that your
> grandfather passed away a year
> ago?

> ROWAN
>
> Yes, my mom's father, but we weren't
> that close.

ROWAN scans the café. Noticing how few customers
there are, she glances at her wristwatch.

ROWAN (cont'd)
I should be going. I have a bus to
catch. It was nice meeting you.

M
You, too. You know, I'd really like
to get together again. It would be
great if we could just get together and talk.

DIRECTOR

And cut.

WRITER

And then, you see, the two of you will continue
to meet for coffee and you'll develop chemistry
and the relationship will blossom. But then there
will be a twist. There is always a twist.

ROWAN

I don't know how I feel about this whole rom-
com thing. It seems disingenuous.

WRITER

Disingenuous? You wound up living with the
guy, so there had to be something about him that
attracted you.

ROWAN

I thought he was a good listener. I thought that
he didn't want anything from me. Man, was I
mistaken.

M
Is that any way to talk about your soulmate?

ROWAN
When are you going to understand that I don't belong to you and I'm not your soulmate?

WRITER
(tapping furiously on laptop)
Okay. Okay. How about we try something else? I know, if this was a crime procedural, M could be the competent but slightly-jaded-by-life police detective who's been set the task of solving a series of assaults on women. Rowan could be the neighbour who lives in the apartment across the hall from where the latest crime took place.

M
Oooh, I like this idea. After all, I was a perfect shot in the police academy. Isn't that right, Rowan?

DIRECTOR
Sounds good to me. Let's run with it and see where it takes us.

ROWAN
You're not giving him a real gun.

WRITER
No. Of course not. I've read over all the notes.

M

Don't believe everything you read ... I guess I'll
be shooting blanks.


ROWAN

And we know how that turned out in real life.
Just ask Dylan. Oh wait, we can't because you
made me have an abortion.


DIRECTOR

Let's focus on the task at hand. People, take your
places ... and action.


**SCENE THREE**
**FADE IN.**
**INT. APARTMENT BLOCK/STAIRCASE — DAY**
An open wooden staircase winds its way up from
the marble foyer of an old ten-storey apartment
building. The building's elevator is currently
out of order. M is a **POLICE DETECTIVE**. He's
wearing a wrinkled suit and is trudging up the
staircase while smoking a cigarette. He stops at
the third floor, putting out his smoke and catching his breath.


POLICE DETECTIVE
I'm getting too old for this shit.


He sighs deeply and keeps slogging up the stairs.


**INT. APARTMENT BLOCK/HALLWAY — DAY**
On the ninth floor is a long hallway with hardwood

floors, oak woodwork, and dimpled stucco walls and ceilings painted a soft cream. Across the doorway to apartment 9B is a gash of bright yellow police tape: "KEEP OUT. CRIME SCENE." The POLICE DETECTIVE knocks on the door to apartment 9C, located directly across from the apartment in which the assault was committed.

THE NEIGHBOUR, a woman in her thirties, answers the door, wearing sweatpants and a long-sleeved T-shirt. A brass chain prevents the door from fully opening.

          THE NEIGHBOUR
  Can I help you?

          POLICE DETECTIVE
  I'm a police detective with the
  special victims unit. We are can-
  vassing the building to see if
  anyone noticed anything unusual
  over the past few days.

          THE NEIGHBOUR
  You mean because of, you know,
  what happened across the hall?

The POLICE DETECTIVE nods.

The chain slowly slides across the bar. THE NEIGHBOUR opens the door to welcome the POLICE DETECTIVE into her apartment, which is decorated with an eclectic mix of thrift-store finds and midcentury modern furniture.

> POLICE DETECTIVE
> Some words of advice. A skimpy brass chain is not going to keep out anyone motivated enough to bust into your apartment.

The POLICE DETECTIVE brushes past THE NEIGHBOUR and into her apartment.

> THE NEIGHBOUR
> Come in, Detective … I'm sorry but I didn't catch your name.

The POLICE DETECTIVE pulls out his ID and shows it to her.

> POLICE DETECTIVE
> You know, you should check iden-tification before inviting some strange man into your apartment.

> DIRECTOR
> And cut. End scene.

> ROWAN
> I don't think that I would have let some strange man into my apartment. That doesn't sound like me.

WRITER

Oh, really. Well, in my research notes it says quite clearly that you were the one who asked M for a kiss. You were the one who invited him into your home.

M

That's true. You were always so trusting.

ROWAN

I let my guard down and I shouldn't have.

WRITER

But you did. It says specifically in my notes, right here on page twenty-three, that after a day spent at his family cottage, he drove you home early the next morning and you asked him for a kiss. He kissed you on the forehead before you embraced for a long time —

ROWAN

I was still intoxicated from the bottles of wine he brought out to the cottage with him. Ordinarily I'm not a drinker.

M

You always were a cheap drunk.

ROWAN

And he was leaving on vacation for six weeks. I felt like I was being abandoned. It was a mistake.

WRITER

Well, that's the understatement of the year.

M

Babe, I would never abandon you — or let you
go. You know that. That's why I always reminded
you of things that needed to change so I wouldn't
divorce you.

ROWAN

Please do me this favour. It's been three and a
half years since I left you and still no divorce.

M

You'll get your divorce when I feel like it. And
right now, I'm not feeling it.

ROWAN

I don't know what it will take for me to be done
with you.

DIRECTOR

You know, I'd like to try out a few more scenar-
ios. Do you have any more ideas?

WRITER

(wringing hands)

Well, if this was a science fiction offering, perhaps Rowan could be a scientist, part of a small
band of resistance fighting against the pod, an
alien hive-mind of plant-life origin that is able
to feed off the memories and consciousness
of their human hosts through a microscopic

parasite released during pollination. M could play a local mathematician, one of the last remaining people left in this college town — one of the lucky few to have escaped exposure to the parasitic organisms and their human hosts.

M

She always was a fan of science fiction. I never understood the attraction, myself.

ROWAN

What about that TV series *V*? You were fascinated by how the aliens who landed on Earth wore human disguises, and how underneath their masks they were of reptilian origin, with plans of dominating humanity and stealing the planet's resources.

M

Like I told you, people wear masks all the time to hide who they really are.

DIRECTOR

All right people, time is money. Let's run with the sci-fi idea and see where it takes us.

SCENE FOUR
FADE IN.
EXT. PUBLIC PARK/CONSERVATORY — NIGHT
A streetlamp illuminates a solitary park bench. The light flickers, casting shadows onto a paved

walkway. A stand of century-old elms secludes
this section of the park. An evening breeze rus-
tles branches, releasing a burst of elm samaras
that skitter along the pathway.

In the shadows is **THE SCIENTIST**. From her covered position, she watches the park bench.
She looks at her watch, the green backlit numbers establishing the time: 11:57 p.m.

                    THE SCIENTIST
          Fuck. Our intel had better be cor-
          rect. I'm in no mood to be wasting
          my time here.

SFX. Footsteps.

**THE MATHEMATICIAN** sits down on the park bench,
holding his satchel on his lap for safekeeping.
He scans his surroundings before placing the
satchel on the ground, directly in front of his
feet.

                    THE SCIENTIST
          Now that's what I'm talking about.

THE SCIENTIST cautiously makes her way out of
the shadows.

                    THE SCIENTIST
          You're late.

THE MATHEMATICIAN
I'm never late. We were supposed
to meet at midnight, and here I
am.

THE SCIENTIST
Not by my watch.

THE MATHEMATICIAN
Well, maybe your watch is broken,
or you just don't know how to read
the time.

THE SCIENTIST
I'm told that you have information
vital to the resistance.

M
(chuckles)
Resistance is futile.

DIRECTOR
Cut!

M
Sorry, I just couldn't resist. And neither could
you, my Tahiti sweetie.

ROWAN
I didn't want to have feelings for you. I tried my
best *not* to have feelings for you.

M
And what did I always tell you?

ROWAN
That you were so lovable I couldn't help but have feelings for you.

DIRECTOR
(sighs)
I should have signed up for a different gig. All right, people, places. Let's give this one another try.

**EXT. PUBLIC PARK/CONSERVATORY — NIGHT**
THE MATHEMATICIAN opens his satchel. He pulls out a file and hands it furtively to THE SCIENTIST.

CLOSE-UP SHOT: The file.

The file contains page after page of paper, all lined with a series of repeating numbers.

THE SCIENTIST briefly scans the file.

THE SCIENTIST
What's this?

THE MATHEMATICIAN
Really, it's a number's game. I've run the computations.

THE SCIENTIST
What computations?

                    THE MATHEMATICIAN
This pestilence, or whatever it
is, is growing exponentially at
an alarming rate.

                    THE SCIENTIST
You're not telling me anything
that we don't already know. This
town is —

                    THE MATHEMATICIAN
I'm not talking about the town.
I'm talking about the entire
planet.

THE SCIENTIST places the file in her backpack.

                    THE MATHEMATICIAN (cont'd)
I've come to the conclusion that
there's no real value to fighting
back.

                    THE SCIENTIST
I don't believe —

                    THE MATHEMATICIAN
We're like the dinosaurs. Unfortunately, our run has come to an end.
It's another species' time to take
the spotlight.

THE MATHEMATICIAN grabs THE SCIENTIST roughly
by the wrist and lets out a guttural bellow, a

sound that is quickly echoed by other hosts in
the vicinity.

> THE SCIENTIST
> What are you doing? Be quiet, for
> God's sake.

> ROWAN
> Wait a minute. Stop.

> DIRECTOR
> Cut! Now what?

> ROWAN
> The script says that she, meaning me, slaps his
> face, hard. So hard that my ring "cuts THE
> MATHEMATICIAN'S cheek, revealing under
> the flap of skin hanging from his face the telltale
> sign of infection: a green mottling of flesh." No
> way would I lay a hand on the guy.

> M
> Well, that's something we can agree on. She
> wouldn't dare.

> WRITER
> (banging head against wall)
> Maybe a horror movie might be closer to the
> truth.

> DIRECTOR
> Well, all I know is that this whole shoot feels like
> a personal nightmare.

> M
>
> She always did have a fascination with vampires.

> WRITER
> (perks up)
> Rowan could play the unsuspecting victim, while M could assume the role of mysterious stranger.

> ROWAN
>
> No kidding, I was the unsuspecting victim in the relationship.

> M
>
> Oh please, don't try playing the innocent with me.

> DIRECTOR
>
> Let's leave all that energy and emotion for the cameras. Places, people. Now, action.

SCENE FIVE
FADE IN.
INT. BLUES BAR — EVENING
A popular blues bar located in Chicago. There's a large sign behind the stage: "LIVE BLUES NIGHTLY." Onstage are a drum kit, a trio of mike stands, and an assortment of guitars. With space being tight, the speakers are suspended from the ceiling. The lighting is dim, made darker by black-painted ceiling tiles. Across from the bar are a dozen bar-height tables, with guests seated on bar stools.

**UNSUSPECTING VICTIM** is drinking with a number of her girlfriends.

> UNSUSPECTING VICTIM
> I think I've had a little too much
> to drink.

> **GIRLFRIEND 1.**
> You've only had a couple of
> margaritas.

> **GIRLFRIEND 2.**
> And the shooters. Don't forget the
> shooters.

> UNSUSPECTING VICTIM
> Ugh, don't remind me.

> GIRLFRIEND 1.
> Remember, what's our motto?

> **ALL**
> Come for the blues. Stay for the
> hangovers.

A **WAITER** approaches their table to drop off a round of drinks.

> UNSUSPECTING VICTIM
> Um, we didn't order these.

> WAITER
> They're on the house. Courtesy of
> that guy.

A **MYSTERIOUS STRANGER**, standing at the end of the bar, raises his beer bottle in toast.

UNSUSPECTING VICTIM leaves the table to use the washroom. There's a lineup.

> UNSUSPECTING VICTIM
> I need some fresh air.

She exits through a door next to the kitchen.

**EXT. ALLEYWAY — NIGHT**
In the alleyway are large trash dumpsters. UNSUSPECTING VICTIM vomits next to one of the dumpsters. The MYSTERIOUS STRANGER is standing outside, in front of the kitchen's closed doorway.

> MYSTERIOUS STRANGER
> Is everything okay? Are you all right?

> UNSUSPECTING VICTIM
> Jesus. You just about scared the crap out of me.

> MYSTERIOUS STRANGER
> Nothing to fear here. I'm one of the good guys.

> UNSUSPECTING VICTIM
> Uh huh. Look, I'm fine. Nothing that a couple of aspirins and half

a gallon of orange juice won't fix.

            MYSTERIOUS STRANGER
I hope that my little offering
back there didn't contribute in
any way toward how you're feeling.

            UNSUSPECTING VICTIM
No worries. Look, I should get
back to my friends.

            MYSTERIOUS STRANGER
Of course. Don't let me keep you.

UNSUSPECTING VICTIM stumbles. The five-inch heel of
one of her shoes has snapped off. The MYSTERIOUS
STRANGER catches her before she face-plants on
hard concrete.

            UNSUSPECTING VICTIM
Thanks for catching me.

            MYSTERIOUS STRANGER
You're welcome. Glad to be of
service.

UNSUSPECTING VICTIM smiles sheepishly.

            UNSUSPECTING VICTIM
Would you mind steadying me?

            MYSTERIOUS STRANGER
Not at all.

The MYSTERIOUS STRANGER extends his arm to
UNSUSPECTING VICTIM. Taking his arm to keep her
balance, she leans down and removes her high
heels. UNSUSPECTING VICTIM studies the broken
heel.

>           UNSUSPECTING VICTIM
>      Well, that was a complete waste
>      of money.

Barefoot, she begins to carefully tiptoe toward
the door.

>           UNSUSPECTING VICTIM
>      Aren't you coming?

>           MYSTERIOUS STRANGER
>      Are you inviting me to join you?

>           UNSUSPECTING VICTIM
>      I'm inviting you to join us.

UNSUSPECTING VICTIM walks toward the bar's entrance. The MYSTERIOUS STRANGER is close behind.
She doesn't catch the momentary glimpse of his
fangs.

>           END SCENE

Today

Today, you will pull back the blankets and crawl out of bed. Today, you will pull back the blankets and crawl out of bed to let the dog out to relieve himself. Today, you will pull back the blankets and crawl out of bed to let the dog out to relieve himself before giving him breakfast. Today, you will pull back the blankets and crawl out of bed to let the dog out to relieve himself before giving him breakfast and you will go to the bathroom: to floss and brush and generally wash up, and dry your hands with a handful of tissues. Today, you will pull back the blankets and crawl out of bed to let the dog out to relieve himself before giving him breakfast and you will go to the bathroom: to floss and brush and generally wash up, and dry your hands with a handful of tissues because the laundry hasn't been done for who knows how many days, which is another task that you ~~should~~ must add to your ever-growing to-do list, that must be recorded once you return to the kitchen with an island and an open view, and stacks of dirty dishes piled high next to the sink. Today you triple pinky-promise to pull back the blankets and crawl out of bed to let the dog out to relieve himself before giving him breakfast before going to the bathroom to floss and brush and generally wash up, before drying your hands with a handful of tissues because clean laundry is lacking because it hasn't been done for who knows how many days, which is another task that you ~~should~~ must add to your ever-growing to-do list, once you return to the kitchen with an island and an open view, and stacks of dirty dishes piled high next to the sink, and have a chai latte and a bowl of muesli kissed with soy milk, which is followed by morning meds because you've been told that consistency and routine are both really important, which then reminds you that today is shower day which always feels like a monumental task, so it's *suck it up, buttercup* as you return to the tiny washroom and turn on the shower allowing the water to warm while you remove your clothing, before climbing into the tub and huddling under the shower head to shampoo and condition greasy locks and to lather up your body with a bar of lavender soap — rinse and repeat, ~~repeat~~ and rinse, repeat before turning off the tap to exit the shower to towel off and to put on your cotton bathrobe with the hole in one pocket before heading to your bedroom where you will try to find within the land mine of dirty clothing something suitable to wear because you have yet to contend with the laundry which presents quite the quandary, *cleanliness is important, is next to godliness*, is part of doing the basics of ~~ADL~~ the Activities of Daily Living you use to rebuild a life that has been broken into fugitive pieces that you lug around each day like chunks of fractured concrete because there's no way to hold back the intrusive thoughts, ~~intrusive thoughts~~ which flash like a strobe ~~lamp~~ light that you try to ignore but can't seem to deflect as you dress because it's like playing a losing game of whack-a-mole, so today you try to distract by ~~sitting down~~ ~~lying down~~ sitting down with your laptop at a desk that you rarely use to try and ~~right~~ write ~~five~~ ~~four~~ ~~three~~ two hundred words for the day which is pretty ~~bad~~ good considering that some hours, days, weeks are more difficult than the rest, you ~~mediate~~ ~~medicate~~ meditate ~~medicate~~ to centre yourself even though all you want to do is lie down in bed to take a nap that lasts forever because every day is as ~~frustrating~~ exhausting as the one just past, which really doesn't matter because now the dog ~~wants~~ needs to go ~~four~~ for a walk which means changing out of your schleps into something more ~~lamentable~~ presentable, not that you really care because the fact is you haven't cared for so very long you can ~~hardly~~ barely ~~rarely~~ remember the last time when you cared, which might prove that M was right when he would tell you that he had a better memory than you did, ~~thoughts~~ a tape which constantly ~~consistently~~ plays on rewind and repeat, rewind and repeat inside your head — that or another one of his Greatest Hits that serenade and loop-de-loop inside your brain, (with a beat) beating you senseless, but the dog stares and doesn't care, okay, well maybe he cares ~~profoundly~~ a little but certainly not as much as he's invested in going for his walk which he reminds you of by barking at every goddamn person he spies through the window and so you place the dog on his leash, put on your Docs and your spring jacket, and then you take him for a walk to and through the neighbourhood park that's a few blocks away from your place while trying not to be annoyed as the dog pulls on the leash, eager to sniff every interesting odour that might come his way as you walk through a tree-lined park before it's time to head back in and take off your shoes and unleash the dog, who runs right in and parks his ninety-five-pound frame upon the couch, and while he barks, you make a lunch because regimens are of great importance and your stomach is growling, so you slap together a sandwich which you eat off the TV tray because you find it uncomfortable to eat meals at the dining room table after all those horrible Sundays spent being lectured by M at your white Ikea dining room table, which now acts as your writing desk where, sometimes, you will sit and write but ~~write~~ right now it is time for lunch while the dog sits on the carpet in front of you and gives the look of *Please, oh pretty please, can I have just one taste?*, which you know you shouldn't, but still do anyways because he's been your constant companion since getting out of your relationship with M, and once you've ~~both~~ had your fill you will ~~try to~~ read a book which will be hit or miss depending on the day, depending on the workings of your brain, a nervous system overload that makes ~~consecration~~ concentration hell, and so you stack the dirty dishes inside the dishwasher, ~~press pots and pans~~, press normal cycle and listen, ~~as~~ another cycle begins, ~~and you go back to that~~ blank page ~~to~~ try ~~cry and~~ finish those ~~five, four, three, two, one hundred~~ words ~~from a few hours ago before you lie down~~ in frustration ~~exhaustion on the sofa bed to~~ answer ~~emails and~~ the call of procrastination ~~before you have~~ to fight a losing battle with heavy eyelids ~~which means that when you awake~~ it's too late ~~to make a meal for yourself, and~~ so ~~you~~ go ahead ~~and place a delivery order of fried rice with tofu and broccoli in a black-bean sauce because you haven't really cook~~ cooked ~~or bake~~ half-baked since ~~you went and left M, and~~ the slog ~~that~~ feels like forever ~~because there's still~~ no ~~divorce or~~ ~~remorse~~ recourse ~~for the harm he has wrought~~ as you turn over in bed thinking, tomorrow, tomorrow, you will get out of bed.

# Thoughts on Keeping a Notebook

> Keepers of private notebooks are a different breed altogether, lonely and resistant rearrangers of things, anxious malcontents, children afflicted apparently at birth with some presentiment of loss.
>
> — Joan Didion, "On Keeping a Notebook"

I didn't keep a diary as a girl. I never filled pages with childhood musings secured by a lock and a tiny brass key. I never possessed a — *for my eyes only, keep out, this means you* — locking pink journal plastered with butterfly-, puppy-, and heart-shaped stickers. During my adolescence, I wasn't one of those teenagers, curled in bed late at night, wearing flannel pyjamas and my emotions on my sleeve, penning the pages of a secret diary kept hidden between a box spring and mattress.

Given my parents' mantras, "Blood is thicker than water" and "Our family does not air our dirty laundry in public," even the thought of keeping a private diary felt like I would be betraying them. A dutiful daughter, I imprisoned my perceptions behind walls of solitary confinement and threw away the key.

*

The wick darkens as my counsellor, Selene, lights the candle. Wax sputters. The candle's flame casts a warm glow of optimism between us. She places a box of tissue on the table (in neutral territory) before asking how my writing has been going. I hold back tears because I haven't written in months. Haven't written because I can't concentrate well enough to write, haven't written because I can't stop thinking about what's happened, what's happening. I haven't written because part of me still believes that I will be breaking M's rule of secrecy. I may have left him, but I'm still not free.

*

M called me a storyteller. It was meant as a compliment — until it wasn't.

*

Selene nudges the box of tissues on the side table toward me. I fight the urge to push it back. "Have you thought any more about my suggestion? About keeping a journal?" Selene says. "Maybe

Writing Prompt #1
Did you come into this world predestined to become a full-fledged
member of some prescient tribe of loss?

_____

_____

_____

_____

_____

_____

_____

_____

_____

Writing Prompt #2
He wrote: "You write deep and rich and well. But I also exist outside
of your imagination. And if I don't then …" Complete the prompt.

_____

_____

_____

_____

_____

_____

_____

_____

_____

writing down your thoughts and feelings will help to open space for your other writing?"

I tell her that keeping a journal feels about as much fun as getting a root canal.

"It can help with the stress, the overwhelm from all the trauma."

I tell her that I don't want to sit with that much pain.

"But aren't you sitting with it already?"

*

M envisioned the life that we would have together. I would be the talented author. He would be the talented therapist, counselling clients in a midcentury modern masterpiece, an idyllic retreat, with ocean views, nestled along the Sunshine Coast. I stopped writing for years, knowing that I couldn't live up to his fantasy. I stopped writing because I was afraid that he would somehow take ownership of my work; that my writing would become about his voice and needs and not mine.

*

I tell Selene that to mark the one-year anniversary of leaving M, I have signed up for an online introductory class to writing creative non-fiction taught by Ayelet Tsabari, a writer whom I have long admired. It's part of a new strategy, registering for online classes and workshops to hopefully help me with my craft. It's also an opportunity to connect with people. It's a challenge taking these courses. I have difficulty with concentration, and it takes additional time for me to process and retain information. One effect of the trauma is that it wreaks havoc on my short-term memory, especially if I'm overwhelmed or overtired. I'm self-conscious because I'm afraid that my scattered thoughts will make me appear foolish in front of other writers and the instructor. I'm concerned that I won't be able to come up with the correct words in conversation;

Writing Prompt #3
Write about a time in your life that stifled your creativity.

_____

_____

_____

_____

_____

_____

_____

_____

_____

_____

Writing Prompt #4
He wrote: "How will you ever manage without me?"

_____

_____

_____

_____

_____

_____

_____

_____

_____

_____

_____

that embarrassing lag between what is heard and what is said. Even so, I'm determined and consider these workshops as acts of self-care seeded like pearls along my path.

*

M told me that I shit diamonds. Translation: All the hurt and harm I had experienced growing up has shaped me into a writer, one who is able to distill past trauma onto the page.

*

The first assignment from Ayelet's non-fiction class is to try a new experience and to write about it. I consider going to a movie by myself or perhaps learning how to refinish the thrift-store dining room table I purchased a few months back so my daughter and I weren't always eating our meals on TV trays in front of the television. "Maybe I'll learn how to make chana masala," I tell Selene. "It's one of my takeout favourites."

But my appetite waxes and wanes, just like my energy level. There are so many options to choose from. Comedy, drama, or sci-fi? Walnut stain or graphite milk paint? I'm terrified of making a mistake — that, somehow, I'll screw things up — thereby proving M's point: that I am incapable of managing my life without him.

*

There was always a right answer and a wrong answer — anything that deviated from his point of view was considered incorrect or an outright challenge to his authority.

*

I research blog posts and essays concerning the keeping of a journal. I read motivational quotes. Face the fear and do it anyways. Lifehacker tries to convince me of a journal's benefits: create a record for posterity; channel creativity; improve your physical

Writing Prompt #5
Write about a new adventure.

_____
_____
_____
_____
_____
_____
_____
_____
_____
_____
_____

Writing Prompt #6
He wrote: "I would never hurt you. You know that, right?"

_____
_____
_____
_____
_____
_____
_____
_____
_____
_____
_____

health and emotional well-being; observe connections and track accomplishments. Just reading the list of possibilities exhausts me.

I search online for guidance, which feels like exploration as well as procrastination. I skim Buzzfeed's "18 Quotes from Famous Writers That Will Make You Want to Start Journaling," which, to be honest, has little effect. The fact is, I don't want to remember what life was like for me during troublesome ages. I'm afraid to excavate and discover what's lurking deep in that dark pit of despair, the one I work so desperately hard not to fall back into; the one in which I sometimes teeter on the edge of; the one whose walls I have roughened bloody as my hands try to claw my way out.

*

For years, M's opinions were to be taken as gospel. He'd say, "You'd be all alone if you left me, Rowan." I worried he was right. I feared I would be alone — forever — if I left him. But it turns out that I wasn't alone. His admonitions and prescriptions came with me. My ever-present and unwanted travelling companions.

*

I walk toward the mall entrance. Valentine hearts plaster the storefront windows. A man strolls out the entrance carrying a bouquet of flowers. I wonder who they're for. Whether it's a romantic gesture or an apology for bruises left behind.

*

I can still feel the pressure of M's grip around my wrist. I shouted no and told him to let go of me. I think that might have been the first and only time that I told him no. He had this look of uncertainty on his face before releasing me. I never told anyone what had happened.

*

Writing Prompt #7
Write about a deep-seated fear.

_____

_____

_____

_____

_____

_____

_____

_____

_____

_____

_____

Writing Prompt #8
He wrote: "Come on, just fucking answer the question!"

_____

_____

_____

_____

_____

_____

_____

_____

_____

_____

_____

Entering my favourite bookstore, I scan for M's presence, a habit I've developed since the separation. All clear, my shoulders relax as I wander toward the shelves displaying journals. I take a meandering route past the new fiction and non-fiction offerings, the anthology, biography, and mythology sections, until I find myself in front of the journals. Nearby there is a display table with Valentine cards, wine glasses, and jewellery.

*

We never celebrated Valentine's Day as a couple. It was an occasion that had made me uncomfortable ever since the age of seven, when my father had given me a fancy heart-shaped box of chocolates while my mother received no gift at all. As for M, he would say, "Let the rest of the masses have Valentine's Day, and we'll take the other three hundred sixty-four to show our love for one another."

*

A trio, deep in conversation, stands a few feet away from me in the bookstore. "I don't like to drive much at night. I can't see a thing in the dark," the man says to his companions, two elderly women with white hair and wizened faces. "But don't tell anybody. It's a secret," he says. "I don't want to get in trouble." I imagine there's a twinkle of delight in his eyes as the women chuckle like teenagers, conspiring to steal their parents' car to go joyriding.

*

How many times did M tell me, "Everyone has secrets. It's how careful we are with them that matters"?

*

Shelves of journals line a section of the back wall at the bookstore. There's a revolving display of metal globes, book lights, scarves, and pens. So many journal options. I consider my pocketbook, and

Writing Prompt #9
Write about a challenge you have faced.

_____
_____
_____
_____
_____
_____
_____
_____
_____
_____
_____

Writing Prompt #10
He wrote: "I'm worried about you. Who do you have in your life besides me?"

_____
_____
_____
_____
_____
_____
_____
_____
_____
_____
_____

how it has been strained since leaving M. He refuses to pay the bills attached to the house and won't agree to putting the bungalow up for sale. The mortgage and house insurance are in my name. I exchange my first choice for a less expensive spiral-bound notebook.

Still, I hesitate with the notebook in my hand. Should I buy it or not? Can I afford it or not? Do I pick lined or unlined pages? What about the size of the notebook? Pocket-sized or scrapbook? It's anxiety provoking. My hands tremble. My mind goes blank. Any instance involving a choice feels problematic, feels life-changingly monumental, and I'm left feeling fucking paralyzed by fear and indecision over a simple notebook.

*

"Party of two," someone announces over the intercom connected to the bookstore's restaurant, Prairie Ink. I watch as a couple heads toward the hostess stand. Briefly, I flash back to my worry that without M in my life, I will be alone — forever. Forever without a partner to share my life and interests with, a lover's intimacy with, a couple's private jokes and building joyful memories with. Alone — forever — except for the trauma like heavy muck on the soles of my shoes that I can't get rid of, and M's admonitions to haunt and taunt me. I take a moment, catch a deep breath, in and out, to contain the potential avalanche of catastrophic thoughts, to remind myself that such may not necessarily be the case in the long term.

*

Once on my own, I slowly started venturing out of the house to attend literary readings. I signed up for writing workshops online and at my treasured bookstore's community classroom. There, I discovered people who were as excited by the written word as I was. I met Ellen, who was writing about her experience of having had eating disorders and whose courage inspired me to pen my own story of leaving and rebuilding my life after domestic abuse.

Writing Prompt #11
Write about a transformational moment in your life.

_____

_____

_____

_____

_____

_____

_____

_____

_____

_____

Writing Prompt #12
He wrote: "You always have to have your story in there. Can't you
ever just listen to mine?"

_____

_____

_____

_____

_____

_____

_____

_____

_____

_____

I met Matt, who was writing a YA novel about a deeply religious young man coming out to his Mennonite family and community; and there was Karla, who wrote poetry coupled with the most beautiful wildlife photography. That nudge into the wider world allowed me to form friendships with writers from across the city.

In a class called "From Experience to Story: Take II," I bonded with a group of women who had also taken prior workshops with our instructor, Marjorie Anderson — a lovely woman, and a writer and editor in her own right, a kind and encouraging mentor. By the end of the session, our intrepid little group made the decision to keep writing and to meet once a month over lunch to talk about our works in progress, as well as about what was happening in our lives.

I also became a part of another writers' group that formed organically from one of Dave Williamson's creative writing classes. Dave, a generous mentor with a number of books to his credit, encouraged me to submit my work. After the workshop was finished, the group began to get together over the occasional lunch to talk about books, the writing craft, and whatever projects we had on the go. My cadre of writing enthusiasts became my good friends. Meeting monthly, we took turns hosting in our homes. We did writing exercises together, shared and critiqued each other's work; often accompanied by a glass of wine and robust conversation.

\*

An extravagance, sure, but even so I leave the bookstore clutching a leather-bound Leuchtturm with hand-stitched binding and acid-free pages lined in grey ink. I decide on my way to my car that I will call my purchase a notebook versus a journal. For some reason it feels less intimidating. I also decide to make it eclectic, by adding hand-drawn sketches, interesting quotes, and my thoughts of being part of a community after so many years of isolation.

Writing Prompt #13
Write about sharing a secret.

_____

_____

_____

_____

_____

_____

_____

_____

_____

_____

Writing Prompt #14
He wrote: "Why does it always have to be about you?"

_____

_____

_____

_____

_____

_____

_____

_____

_____

*

Via social media, I met writers, both emerging and established, from across the globe, people who generously and genuinely welcomed me into their creative fold.

An online course with Rachel Thompson, a writer who radiates warmth, led me to a community of writers who celebrate each other's writing, as well as their submission successes and failures.

Through online courses offered by Nicole Breit, I found my way into writing creative non-fiction and finally discovered my voice. My pieces languishing in a drawer could finally be shaped into the stories I needed to tell. I began using novel forms that meshed with the way my brain worked as a tangential thinker and trauma survivor. Memoir as essay worked by stitching fragments of time-scattered memories into a patchwork of creation that was coherent and hopefully beautiful. Having a supportive framework gave me the opportunity to reshape uncomfortable events from raw material to polished writing. Pushing against traditional narratives reminded me of the discipline and freedom found in John Coltrane's jazz or Jackson Pollock's paintings.

Of equal importance was that I finally discovered other writers who were as interested in these forms as I was. These were the people who worked diligently on their craft, who were as captivated by the beauty of a well-written phrase as I was. These were the people who embraced me as a writer, who were willing to workshop and share ideas, who were pushing the boundaries of essay and memoir. There was more than one way to legitimately tell a story. I had finally discovered my community of creative rebels.

*

I make the commitment to write in the morning after having breakfast. I set up my writing space in my closet of a bedroom and light the creativity candle given to me at Winter Solstice by one of my daughter's friends from high school — someone I consider

Writing Prompt #15
Try something new and write about it.

_____

_____

_____

_____

_____

_____

_____

_____

Writing Prompt #16
Write about an experience of joy.

_____

_____

_____

_____

_____

_____

_____

_____

family. The pen in my hand holds sentimental value. It was given to me at Solstice by my youngest daughter, Annabella, who is a connoisseur of paper and pen. I finally understand what she means: that tactile sensation of ink moving with ease onto the page.

\*

The presence of a writing community in my life cheered me on whenever I felt like I just couldn't face another day. Our shared passion for writing was a boon to my soul; the act of writing became my distraction, my passion, my lifeline.

\*

The flame flickers and casts a soft glow. The air fills with the scent of vanilla and undertones of tobacco. I feel resistance rising as I pick up my pen. It's difficult to write when someone you once trusted turns the word *storyteller* into something shameful. It's difficult to write when someone you once trusted uses the word *storyteller* as a way to insinuate that you have no concept of reality. It's difficult to write when the word *storyteller* has been used as a weapon to destroy any thoughts and perceptions that didn't coincide with his own. I repeat the candle's mantra, *Creativity is flowing through me*, as I sink into my thoughts and memories, the comfort of oversized pillows. I write about a man carrying flowers, a couple rushing down the aisle, my gratitude for being a part of a writing community, and my appreciation for becoming a keeper of a notebook.

Writing Prompt #17
What does freedom look like to you?

_____

_____

_____

_____

_____

_____

_____

_____

_____

_____

_____

_____

_____

_____

_____

_____

_____

_____

_____

_____

_____

_____

_____

_____

## A Map of the World

No map can be a perfect representation of reality; every map is an interpretation.

— Casey Cep, "The Allure of the Map," *New Yorker*

## A GLOSSARY OF TERMS

**Leaver** (noun) *leav-er*. Definition: one who hits the road, the happy trail, who makes tracks.

**Leavee** (also noun) *leav-ee*. Definition: the one left behind, who never saw it coming.

I told you that I loved you. You told me that I'd be the one to leave. That I wouldn't be able to help myself, as if it was part of my DNA. You said, "Babe, you've always been the leaver in a relationship and not the leavee."

 **LEGEND**

 My ancestors sailed across the Atlantic in ships bound for the New World. Some came by choice. Others came bound in chains. They left loved ones behind in rural villages in Poland and Great Britain, were torn from family and the familiar on the West African continent. Their voices echo down the halls of Ellis Island, New York; the cobblestone walkways of Halifax; the squalid slave quarters of South Carolina. Their voices rise from the pages of the *Book of Negroes*. I am the daughter of diasporas.

My father's family had a saying: "Blood is thicker than water." There were so few people of colour living in Winnipeg at that time, I think we clung to one another out of desperation.

"People like to think that it's bad only in the States," Grandma Daisy said. "But up here it's just as prejudiced. Worse." She would have married the devil himself if that would have taken her away from the racism in Truro, Nova Scotia.

Grandpa Lever left South Carolina after his brother was beaten to death with a hammer for applying for a white man's job. Part of the Great Migration, he settled in Chicago before immigrating to Canada. No mention was made of his family left behind.

As a child, Grandma Frances was abandoned by her mother. She was raised by male relatives on a family farm in Cooks Creek, Manitoba, while her sister, Violet, lived elsewhere with their mother.

My mother's parents packed their bags, ready to go. They moved to California, crossed a border we couldn't unless my father stayed behind and my brothers and I pretended we were Spanish. A pretense my mother refused to have us follow.

Grandma Frances would call us, out of the blue, to pick her up from the Greyhound bus depot. She left Grandpa Mike and his whisky bottle behind in California more times than I can remember.

There were elevations and depressions in the landscape. Mother had more lows than highs. Born during the Great Depression, she took it too much to heart.

Father kept a small duffle bag next to the back door. He would grab that bag and say he was heading to the gym. But he wasn't fooling anyone.

##  *TERRA INCOGNITA*

Latin for "lands unknown." In ancient times, people believed the world was flat. That if they ventured too far, they would fall off the edge of the world, into an abyss where mythical creatures and monsters dwelled. *Hic sunt dracones* — Here be dragons.

During my childhood, my mother instructed me to stay in the backyard, where it was safe. She often said, "The world will screw you just as soon look at you." Still, I wandered from home because I refused to believe that the outside world was as horrific a place as my mother purported it to be.

On my way to elementary school, I'm stopped by a red light on the corner. A man pulls over in his car, leans across to open the passenger door, and offers me a ride, one that I decline. His eyes are black holes, cold and lifeless — just like my father's.

*Hic sunt dracones.* Here be monsters after all.

You wanted to show me the world, a way forward, love. When we first met, you said that you didn't want anything from me. You held me in your arms, and I felt safe. Back then, you were such unfamiliar territory. I think that feeling of safety was something I'd been searching for all my life. It was a potent drug, more magical than any elixir.

##  COMPASS

I know, we're polar opposites, but I couldn't help but love you.

I grew compass roses in my cottage garden just so they bloomed in your direction. We followed a trail of scarlet rose petals as if we were navigating our way through a fairy-tale wood. I wonder, was it ever really possible for us to find our way out of the forest — you know, the one we couldn't see for the trees? You were a Boy Scout, once upon a time, but I don't think it helped. And me? I had really bad astigmatism and a lousy sense of direction. Still, didn't you love how our bodies bumped and collided as we walked down the perennial aisles of the garden centre on our way to say *I do*?

## ✦ IMAGINARY LINES

At ten, I'm bloody knees, bumps, and bruises. My teachers call me the girl who trips over snowflakes and imaginary lines as I dodge bullies and taunts of "nigger" on the playground.

At twelve, I'm round ass and recent developments. I stumble over the fault line drawn through my childhood as my mother, inconsolable at the thought of her husband leaving, begs me to convince him to stay.

At thirteen, I'm called down to the office to talk to the school nurse, who wants to know how things are at home. I don't say a word because who would believe me? After all, my mother says nothing happened. From her perspective, I'm just a drama queen, reciting imaginary lines.

## ✦ CARTOGRAPHY

Conjugal visits. Conjugate the past. I lie. We lie. He/she lies. They lie.

Somewhere lies the open road, the promised land.

During my childhood, I lie in bed beneath a canopy of glow-in-the-dark stars, counting footsteps. Creating maps in my head out of need, travelling through open windows, across ridgelines, under power lines, over neglected lawns and flower beds filled with peonies — bleeding hearts — under rotting picket fences, down back lanes connected to streets leading to high ways, and bye ways.

You and I lie in bed, in your apartment beneath a blue half-moon sculpted from fibreglass attached to the wall. Your hands, your tongue, are expedition parties mapping desires and betrayals along the contours of my body. Some body. We play Marco Polo with my past as I float on the ceiling and watch you fuck me.

In group, we survivors yield to the past, exhausted by detours. There's no more lying to ourselves. Keeping secrets. We map our emotions with brand new packs of crayons smelling of innocence. We create internal havens hidden from the rest of the world. We summon safe spaces, real or imagined, to calm neural pathways of guilt and shame, arterial thoroughfares of terror.

On paper-doll cut-outs we colour the emotions that lurk and surge like electricity beneath the surface. Giving shape to the fears and tears and rage we cannot give voice to by ourselves. Arts and crafts for adult survivors of intimate partner violence.

| KEY: | |
|---|---|
| Shame ++++++++++<br>++++++++++ | Fear <<<<<<<<<<<<<<<<<br><<<<<<<<<<<<<< |
| Hyperarousal #######<br>####### | Tension *************<br>************* |
| Numbness . . .<br>                 shade areas<br>No Feeling . . . | Guilt ^^^^^^^^^^^<br>^^^^^^^^^^^ |
| Anger !!!!!!!!!!!!!!!!!!!!!!!!!! | Sadness SSSSSSS |

### ◈ ATLAS

Shrugged — a lot.

While travelling, a sense of humour is important. So are snacks and good company, as well as an awesome playlist.*

Sometimes I imagine heading to parts unknown — driving in my car until I run out of cash or am stopped by the ocean. I'll pick up hitchhikers along the way. Maya Angelou will ride shotgun and choose the music, while in the back seat Mary Magdalene will take selfies with Frida Kahlo and Persephone. We'll leave a trail of Hot Rod and Twizzlers wrappers, empty cans of Pringles Originals and Diet Coke, and du Maurier cigarette butts in our wake.

### ◈ POLARIS

The Big Dipper. The Drinking Gourd. How many lost their way following that North Star to freedom?

We huddled on the beach beneath a cemetery of dead suns. You pointed the way toward Polaris. True north. True love. You told me we'd grow old together. That when the time came, your spirit would wait for me on the North Star. You said, "Our souls are bound for all eternity. We'll be together always."

### ◈ KEY

◉━ Words and phrases used to describe symbols on a map as a means to assist with navigation, interpretation. Key symbols. I've got that good hair and would pass that paper bag test, every time. Words and phrases. Whore. Madonna. Daddy's little girl — the one nobody loves, according to Mother. Exotic other, tragic mulatto, too-white-to-be-a-black girl. Not a woman but a woman of colour. A shapeshifter like Ray Bradbury's Martian, Tom, just trying to survive in the world.

---

* See page 124.

🔑 Pregnant at nineteen, I leave home and move in with my boyfriend, R. Father does his own disappearing act and shacks up with his latest mistress, while Mother has a nervous breakdown. U-turn. Back home I care for my mother, my brothers, my boyfriend, our newborn baby. I tell my mother that I have no intentions of marrying: "I want to concentrate on being a good mom and completing university." My mother calls me a user, just like my father.

🔑 After the wedding, I cry, knowing it was a mistake. A mistake — my father's response when I decide two years later to have another baby. "Have an abortion," he tells me. "You don't want to wind up some fat slob pumping out babies on welfare." A year after birthing and bringing my newborn daughter home, I begin starving myself and working out at the gym. A few months later I end my marriage. A few years later I graduate from university with two degrees and a full-blown eating disorder.

🔑 On our first date, H removes the ceiling fixture illuminating my kitchen and cleans it at the sink. "Look how much you need me around here," he says. When he moves in, he brings his musical aspirations, amp, and keyboards. He says he's a light traveller since dealing with all of his baggage in AA.

Things go from bad to worse, to black and blues; from biting my tongue and biding my time to clandestine phone calls to friends, to eventually finding the courage to leave him. I pack a few belongings for myself and my children while he's at rehearsal. But I get no dress rehearsal before leaving, as he confronts me at the door.

### ✦ ELEVATION

You put me on a pedestal. I wish you hadn't. It's a long way down. And while I might enjoy the view, the peaks, the perks, and may survive the inevitable fall, I'm doubtful about the landing.

### ✦ INTERSECTION

Meet you, M, at the crossroads. We'll make pacts with the devil, just like Robert Johnson. See you, maybe, baby, at the junction of gender and racial bias, the XXX marks the spot of fucked-up family history, free will, and destiny.

There's a teenage girl with dreadlocks, torn jeans, and faded T-shirt, begging on the boulevard of broken promises, next to the intersection of Grant and Pembina Highway. I wonder if she is like me. If we share similar histories, that one-in-three statistic. Questions that go through my mind as I pull over in my car, roll down the window, and give her a twenty-dollar bill, hoping she'll find her way. There but for the grace of yada yada — you get the idea. I understood on some level why she chose the streets over home. I would have, too, but I was afraid of being such an easy target at sixteen. So I stayed and developed other escape routes. When autumn comes, she'll head west down the Trans-Canada Highway, most likely craving sunshine and safety, Skittles, and the semblance of family.

### ✦ BOUNDARY MARKERS

Objects set on the ground to preserve and pinpoint the location of boundaries.

My body was virgin territory, surrounded by steep walls made of blankets and stuffed animals.

### ✦ RELIEF

Topographical. Medicinal. Physical. Emotional. Spiritual. Disaster.

"Stop making mountains out of molehills."

Diana Ross was fierce. There wasn't a mountain high enough, valley low enough, or river wide enough to keep her from her man.

I never learned to drive stick. You tried to teach me, but apparently I "can't be taught." On road trips, you were always the driver, while I wrestled old school with CAA maps and tried to point us in the right direction. We played travel games in the car like Would You Rather?, Who'd You Rather?, Fortunately/Unfortunately, and Twenty Questions. That one wasn't my favourite because it felt like an interrogation. On our first trip through the States, we drove through Glacier National Park on the Going-to-the-Sun Road. We crossed the Continental Divide on a two-lane road so high in the mountains that we played peek-a-boo in the clouds.

### ◈ BORDER CROSSINGS

My family tree's split down the middle and divided by a border. Too Black. Too white. Sometimes just right. I have white cousins in California that I'll never meet and Black cousins back home in Canada who tell me that I'm lucky because I can pass, as if hiding in plain sight is some kind of blessing.

After Mass, there's a family drive followed by dinner at my paternal grandparents. My father's childhood home is in the North End, across the Louise Bridge spanning the Red River. As the bridge comes into sight, I hold my breath, cross my fingers, and pray, convinced that if I don't, a hole will materialize and our car will plummet into the river. At six, I've taken it upon myself to save my family.

*Romper Room* and race riots broadcast daily in black and white. The narrative teaches me as a child about the vulnerability of brown and Black bodies. I watch enraged mobs of white people attack peaceful protestors. I witness the aftermath of church bombings, parents crying out for their murdered children. Fear becomes my travelling companion.

### ◈ DEGREES

Of latitude and longing.

I yearn for places somewhere over the rainbow. My favourite movie is *The Wizard of Oz*, even though I'd have taken a hard pass on Dorothy's ruby red slippers.

I'm four, the first time that I run away. My parents find me thirteen blocks from home, sitting in the bleachers, eating popcorn and watching a baseball tournament at the community club. Father calls me his happy wanderer. Mother calls me stubborn and willful, and drags me kicking and screaming home.

We fell in and out of love imperceptibly, incrementally, by varying degrees.

49.8916° N, 97.1545° W: We sat and talked for hours about life, the universe, and everything in between. After I told you I was afraid of H, do you remember what you said? You told me to trust my instincts, to listen to that fear. You gave me permission to heed that little voice inside my head whispering misgivings. But in the end, you wanted that permission slip back.

50.708901° N, 96.564064° W: Your cosmic spot. Your sacred space. We drank wine under a starry sky and fell in love.

49.9494° N, 97.1519° W: Our favourite booth, hours of conversation over coffee and cigarettes. The staff knew we were a couple before I did.

51.126887° N, 115.388345° W: Our cabin in the woods. We couldn't keep our hands off one another. I couldn't keep the panic attacks at bay while I supposedly healed the sexual shame inside you.

44.224199° N, 103.376605° W: You had too much to drink and became angry with me during dinner. You insisted on driving while intoxicated. There was nothing I could say.

40.7529° N, 73.98338° W: I sat on the hardwood floor, in tears, beside the bed while you accused me of having an affair.

18.729019° N, 68.460905° W: Our last night, we strolled the beach, a last attempt at a romantic gesture. A security guard walked past carrying an automatic rifle. Maybe it was a sign.

48.858822° N, 2.337755° E: A bridge covered in lovers' locks. Crossing the Pont des Arts in Paris, France, we barely speak. We do not touch.

How was it that I missed the hazard signs along the way?

## ◈ POINTS OF INTEREST

Points of interest — point of views. Lookout spots.

From your perspective, I'm your hero, soulmate, lover. Your favourite storyteller … a profound disappointment … a teller of tall tales, who sees you as some secondary character, who in the recounting will only get it wrong. I'm Parthenope, a maiden-voiced siren with café-au-lait skin and Beyoncé-long braids who seduced you with my song as I floated, supported by hot-pink Styrofoam noodles, in suburban in-ground swimming pools.

## ◈ SCALE

From my perspective, you distorted reality like a Mercator projection.

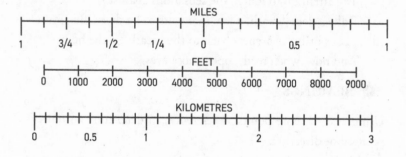

*Give an inch. Take a mile.*

## ◈ ORIENTATION

I'm in the throes of a flashback, a step back, a remembrance of times past, a brief passage of time since I've left M. I speak with Tara from the crisis line, who wants to know, "Are you safe?" *Yes.* "Where are you right now?" *Living room.* Who reminds me to breathe. *Can't.* Who asks me to concentrate. "Tell me three things you see." *Couch. Rug. Chair.* "Three things you hear?" *Furnace. Train. Dog.* "Three things you feel?" And panic's engine revs. I sit, stand, sit, pace, sit, my body Novocain numb.

Tara guides me through the exercise, over and over again. *Couch. Rug. Chair. Furnace. Train. Dog. Orange couch. Rug. Chair. Train whistle. Furnace humming. Dog.* Teasing out details ... *orange linen couch ... midcentury modern chair ...* until I can feel the nubby cords of shag carpet beneath my bare feet, my body's weight on the sofa, the softness of my dog's coat against my palm.

A grounding exercise. "Think about a space, a place real or imagined, where there's the sensation of being at ease. Safe. Picture being there now. What is the setting? Describe textures ... colours ... objects. Concentrate.

"Focus on what is heard.

"What is smelled.

"How does it feel to be there?

"Pay attention to touch, the sensations against skin.

"Take a deep breath, a few moments to be there. Be grounded ... Let's bring awareness back to the breath ... the body.

"And now, when ready, open those eyes."

### ✦ BEARINGS

Using two or more points as reference, to determine an object's position or direction.

My domestic-abuse counsellor, Donna, says the decision to leave the situation is scary. It's a journey into the unknown. A trust walk. She says it's like standing in front of a long, dark tunnel carved through a mountain. There is a glimmer of light at the opposite end. And even though it's frightening, the only way through is forward. Break it down,

step

by

step.

No one should have to do this alone.

It was you and me, babe. It was us against the world — until it wasn't.

Cardinal directions. Cardinal points. Cardinal rules — there were so many. I tried to follow them and lost my way. Why were the points of reference always yours? North. South. East. West. I wanted to be the one who loved you best, believe me. Will anyone believe me?

Bearings: A fixed position. Yours. Mine. Proceed with caution.

A note tacked on a picture frame, letting you know why I had left, but not where I had gone. The road to Hell was a one-way yellow-brick road paved with good intentions. Please believe me, this was not me taking the easy way out, the path of least resistance. Bear in mind, I wanted to tell you. But I couldn't. Because of roadblocks. Because I was afraid of you. I lost my voice as well as my way. I would have burned you a CD of sad songs, but I was pressed for time. Besides, you never liked my taste in music.

Bearings: I'm afraid I will never find mine, that this pain is permanent — fixed. Ahead lies rocky terrain and I'm scared of stumbling the rest of my life.

To quell the fear and anxiety, I walk the dog down unfamiliar streets and sidewalks, counting steps, one foot in front of the other. Tiny steps. Baby steps. Mindful steps. One step forward, two steps back — until fear starts to thaw like the snow on my path, until I can hear the hopeful call of Canada geese overhead, until I feel the breeze of the north wind gust against my face, until I can find my way home.

## A MAP OF THE WORLD: PLAYLIST
21 songs. 1 hour, 35 minutes

"Little Red Corvette" — Prince
"Fast Car" — Tracy Chapman
"Highway to Hell" — AC/DC
"Radar Love" — Golden Earring
"Reverend Jack and His Roamin' Cadillac Church" — Timbuk 3
"Mustang Sally" — The Commitments
"Killer/Papa Was a Rollin' Stone" — George Michael
"Love Me Like a Man" — Bonnie Raitt
"Crossroads" (live) — Cream
"Crossroad Blues" — Robert Johnson
"Under Pressure" — Queen & David Bowie
"Sweet Dreams (Are Made of This)" — Marilyn Manson
"Personal Jesus" — Depeche Mode
"Wicked Game" — Chris Isaak
"Standing Outside a Broken Phone Booth with Money in My
    Hand" — Primitive Radio Gods
"Ventura Highway" — America
"Should I Stay or Should I Go" — The Clash
"Everyday Is a Winding Road" — Sheryl Crow
"Graceland" — Paul Simon
"Freedom! '90" — George Michael
"Birmingham" — Amanda Marshall

**Forest, Tree, Branch, Root**

*You don't ask if the names of the interview rooms at the Crisis Response Centre are intentional. You don't ask if the names were chosen to offer reassurance to those who are currently unable to find solace in Mother Nature — or in anything else for that matter. Named after trees, there is the oak room; there is the birch. There are the aspen, the elm, the maple, the ash, the willow, and the cedar rooms. You can't help but wonder if this is some kind of insider's cosmic joke, one of those reminders that you can't see the literal forest for the trees?*

1. Amur Maple: *Acer ginnala*
Height: 20 feet (6 metres)
Spread: 25 feet (8 metres)
Sunlight: ⭘ full sun ◑ part shade
Hardiness Zone: 2a
Description and Observations: The Amur maple has an attractive grey-brown bark that is smooth on young branches

but becomes fissured with age. The dark green leaves of this multi-stemmed tree or large shrub turn flame red in autumn. It reproduces by releasing a multitude of samaras.

🍃 The only tree that wouldn't grow in your garden on Coralberry Avenue was the Amur maple given to you by your mother as a birthday gift — before you were cut off from your parents and siblings. Despite soil amendments, buckets of iron chelate, your efforts were for naught. The leaves faded from green to barely there yellow before dropping to the ground. Your best efforts, which included consultation with an arborist, couldn't keep that tree alive. You wept when it died; grieved when you had to have it removed from your garden, where other trees, shrubs, and perennials thrived.

*The interview rooms at the Crisis Response Centre are used for counselling and assessment, to determine whether time and a session of counselling are sufficient or if a stay in the Crisis Stabilization Unit or the psychiatric ward of the hospital is warranted. You're relegated to a pumpkin-coloured vinyl chair in the oak room. The walls are painted gingersnap and decorated with brown canvas panels and Impressionist paintings. You study an oak leaf painting. Or, at least, try to, because your eyelids are swollen to slits and the world looks as if you are viewing it from under water — which seems fitting — because at this moment you feel like you're drowning. You're exhausted by the undertow after leaving M. You sit across from a crisis support worker, a woman in her sixties with a kind face and a kinder tone, wearing John Lennon–style frames that she peers over when she talks. When you talk. When she suggests that you spend a few days at the CSU, the in-patient Crisis Stabilization Unit, because your complex post-traumatic stress disorder has been triggered by recent events with M and is on high and self-harming alert. When, reluctantly, you agree to go for your safety and well-being.*

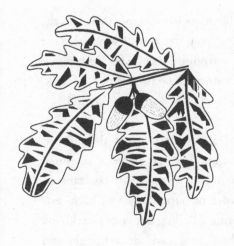

2. Burr Oak: *Quercus macrocarpa*
Height: 80 feet (24 metres)
Spread: 80 feet (24 metres)
Sunlight: ◐ full sun
Hardiness Zone: 2
Description and Observations: Tolerant of poor soil conditions, the burr oak can live to be three hundred years old. Native to the prairie landscape, it is a heritage tree for future generations. Its distinct lobed leaves turn yellow come fall. Difficult to transplant and sensitive to environmental changes, burr oaks prefer well-drained soil.

On Sundays during your childhood, your family piled into the car for a scenic drive along Scotia Street to Kildonan Park. Entering through the southeastern gate, you sometimes imagined that all thirty-nine hectares of parkland belonged to you and that the people milling about were your guests. Summers, your parents started up the charcoal barbecue, and you'd have a picnic. After the feast, you and your brothers would cross an expanse of manicured lawn and a short wooden bridge to visit the Witch's Hut, nestled within the trees. During autumn, you collected and pressed scalloped-edged oak leaves between the pages of books for school projects. You watched as squirrels squabbled over acorns collected and stockpiled in secret stashes for survival. Winters, you hurled down the park's toboggan slides or laced up and skated, surrounded by the sentinels of trees next to the frozen duck pond. When bored with playing crack the whip or your feeble attempts at figure skating, you'd enter the skating path on the creek that meandered its way beneath the bridge leading to the Witch's Hut.

When it was time to pack up the skates to go home, there was the *kthunk kthunk* of skate guards as you tottered your way inside the pavilion and downstairs to the warming benches. Spring brought you back to Kildonan Park, to witness the return of bud, of stalk, of leaf, of sapling: the continuous circle of death and renewal.

At fifteen, you discovered a sanctuary across the railroad tracks, a few blocks from your family's new home. Centennial Park was your retreat from your parents and their constant arguing. You'd sit within the grove of burr oaks, your back resting against a rough and scaly trunk. Pulling out your sketchbook and charcoal sticks, you'd light a smoke and draw upright and horizontal branches. You appreciated the quiet, the calm, as you whiled away the time drawing oak after oak.

When M left his marriage, he moved into an apartment building located on the opposite side of the Red River facing Kildonan Park. At times, you'd imagine him standing on the balcony to his apartment late at night, smoking a cigarette, drinking wine or a few bottles of beer, looking toward your home and fantasizing about fucking you.

*The birch interview room is painted a warm grey, and there are chestnut canvas panels attached to the walls. The furniture is heavy and, you expect, difficult to toss, although you're not the kind of person who will test the theory out — anger being an emotion that you find difficult to express. The tables are round, no sharp corners or hard angular edges; check off the childproofing for adults. On the wall opposite to where you huddle in a chair, hugging a warm blanket for comfort, you can't help but notice the ominous figures lurking within the Modernist painting of a birch forest. There is the grim-jawed man in grey; the child intently peeling a green apple with a metal corer; the petrified figure, back pressed against a tree; the large man, hiding in the forest like the wolf from "Little Red Cap."*

3. Birch: *Betula* "Crimson Frost"
Height: 25–40 feet (8–12 metres)
Spread: 15–25 feet (5–8 metres)
Sunlight: ⭕ full sun ◖ part
shade
Hardiness Zone: 4–7
Description and Observations:
An accent tree, upright and oval
with deep purple leaves and pen-
dulous branches. The peeling
bark is white with flecks of cinnamon. Tolerates poor soil conditions yet tends not to perform
well in clay soil.

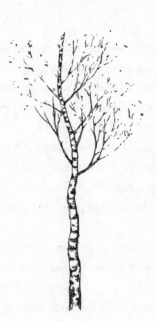

The landscaper said that he had never seen a pair of Crimson
Frost birch as healthy and thriving as the ones you had planted in
your front yard.

When Beth decided to marry, you fashioned garlands made
from hemp cord and trimmed bundles of birch and red osier dogwood twigs cut from your garden. They brought a remembrance
of home to the festivities. They festooned the wedding aisle, the
rustic wooden canopy draped with swaths of lace that overlooked
rolling hills, creek, and farmland, with the Rocky Mountains in
the background.

You didn't want M at your daughter's wedding. You didn't
want to sit beside him during the ceremony, stand next to him in
the family photographs taken with the bride and groom. You didn't
want to be with him at the reception, where he blamed you for not
having prepared a speech despite your daughter's email reminders
to him. You didn't want to look up from the podium to see his face

smouldering red-hot disapproval as you gave a toast in honour of the newly married couple. You didn't want to share his bed, acknowledge the remortgage documents he'd been pressuring you to sign that he'd left on your pillow like a love letter. You didn't want to smell the alcohol on his breath, feel the heat of his body as he leaned in close during the speeches and laughed softly before whispering in your ear, "Maybe I should tell them how the two of us got together." "Go ahead," you told him, challenging his authority. He didn't respond. He just poured himself another glass of wine.

*Waiting to be transferred to the CSU, you're thankful you've been relocated from the oak room to the birch, which is situated farther down the hallway. You're indifferent to the recliner's change of colour from nut brown to khaki. But you're appreciative of the additional distance from the man relegated to the interview room next to the oak; the balladeer, you call him, with his constant, off-key serenade of Beatles, Queen, and Debbie Harry singles belted out at the top of his lungs. You're a staunch Blondie fan, but hearing some man singing that he's going to track you down and get you no matter what does not help your situation any.*

4. Trembling Aspen (White Poplar): *Populus tremuloides*
Height: 82 feet (25 metres)
Spread: 16 feet (5 metres)
Sunlight: ◯ full sun
Hardiness Zone: 1
Description and Observations:
A fast-growing tree, native to Manitoba. The leaves are reminiscent of heart shapes that quiver under the slightest of breezes. Trembling aspen propagates by a suckering root system that

produces clonal colonies. The bark is light grey with horizontal striations.

🍃 Your father planted a trembling aspen next to the crabapple tree in your backyard, located in the working-class neighbourhood of East Kildonan. Initially, the house had belonged to one of your mother's relatives. Your parents purchased the house as a rent-to-own; as an interracial couple, finding a home without such intervention would have been near impossible at that time.

🌿 M called aspens "weed trees." He said that they were nothing but a pain in the ass, becoming uprooted during storms at the cottage because of their shallow root system. Still, you liked the sound their heart-shaped leaves made as they quivered in the breeze, clattering like tiny castanets.

*You think this is your third visit to the Crisis Response Centre since you physically left M. Perhaps it is the fourth. Perhaps. It's difficult to remember the simplest of things while your thoughts are pulled like metal filings toward him and the magnitude of the harm that he has wrought. It's exhausting, the process of removing the twisted tangle of imprinted messages he has implanted within your brain over the years you were with him; the ones that have taken root and reign and creep beneath your skin like a telltale sign from a B horror movie — an invasion of the body snatchers — shifted blame that germinated into invasive suckers.*

5. Peachleaf Willow: *Salix amygdaloides* Anderss
Height: 35–50 feet (11–15 metres)
Spread: 50 feet (15 metres)
Sunlight: ⭘ full sun ◑ part sun
Hardiness Zone: 4
Description and Observations:
A medium-sized tree. Native to Manitoba,

peachleaf willows have an extensive root system that makes them ideal for the prevention of riverbank erosion. Can be found alongside rivers and lakes and in swampy, wooded areas.

 As a child, you thought that the name weeping willow was just so sad. You were like that as a child, empathic to the point where walking past your neighbour's weeping willow would bring on a twinge of pain.

*You wish the overstuffed, khaki-coloured, pseudo-La-Z-Boy contraption operated as a genuine recliner. A genuine recliner would come in handy after you'd been crying for three hours plus. You're seriously past the cusp of exhaustion and overwhelm as you try to ignore the ballad-eer's Barbara Walters and Frank Sinatra impersonations. When he sings "Under Pressure," you can't help but think,* No fucking kidding.

6. American Elm: *Ulmus americana*
Height: 98 feet (30 metres)
Spread: 50 feet (15 metres)
Sunlight: ◑ full sun ◐ part shade
Hardiness Zone: 2a
Description and Observations:
Native to Manitoba. Winnipeg is home to the largest concentration of elms in North America. The foliage is dark green, turning golden in the fall. The bark is ridged and dark ashy grey. It propagates by releasing an abundance of seeds, called samaras, that are surrounded by papery discs.

After you left M, you lived in a tiny two-bedroom bungalow on

Telfer Street, with a sun porch overlooking the elms. Having transformed the sunroom into a writing space, you'd sit at your desk, drawing inspiration and a sense of calm from watching the scenery outside. Early summer, those elm samaras burst from the trees like bushels of snow set loose from the clouds. You thought of the elm tree in front of the home that was yours but no longer yours, how the seeds fell and lodged between interlocking brick and crushed granite mulch, and the hours you spent mindfully plucking tiny seedlings out by hand.

While living in this rental home, you walked your dog to the park next to Omand's Creek. The walks were challenging at times — whenever you spied plants from the garden you'd had no choice but to leave behind, you wanted to weep.

Oftentimes you did weep at the remembrance of what was lost. The yellow brightness of Stella D'Oro daylilies, the aromatic scent of Adelaide Hoodless rose bushes, the Karl Foerster feather reed grass that swayed under the gentlest of breezes, all planted by hand, your spade digging in the richness of clay soil amended with cow manure and nutrient-rich mulch. Because the move from Coralberry Avenue was so rushed, you never had time to properly say goodbye to your garden, a place of healing that teemed with life.

You followed a meandering path that led to a bridge tied with red ribbons, symbolic reminders of this nation's murdered and missing Indigenous women and girls. Past the bridge, there was an elm with a huge burl that looked like the open maw of a gargoyle standing guard.

There came a time when your second ex-husband, H, would hide behind the elm tree across the street from where you lived.

With custody of your youngest still undecided, he lurked on Sundays as you packed your toddler into the car for an afternoon of exploration and play at Kildonan Park.

Encircled by a stand of elms, you and your daughter played on the swing sets and slides at the very same playground you remembered from your childhood. You bought Popsicles from the concession stand next to the playground. Later, with lips stained cherry red, you'd take your daughter for a short walk, often stopping by the duck pond to watch the ducks as they frolicked in the water; often crossing the wooden bridge that led to a fairy-tale rendering of the witch's house from "Hansel and Gretel."

There were times you tempted fate and walked your dog late at night through the park next to the creek, beneath the dim glow of streetlamps and the shadows of elms, not caring if any harm might come your way.

It was a spring day when the elm in your rental home's backyard was cut down to a stump. Your neighbour had purchased a new vehicle and didn't want any debris from the tree landing on her car. She complained to the landlord. It was painful watching the elm destroyed for the sake of a newer-model vehicle. With so much of your history lost to diasporas, you thought, as you considered the day-to-day events the tree had born witness to over its lifespan of one hundred years, how careless people are with the past that surrounds them. It pained you to watch the sparrows lined up in confusion on your wooden fence, their beaks holding insects to feed their fledglings sacrificed when the elm was removed.

In Greek and Roman mythology, dryads were nymphs who lived in trees and perished when their trees died or were cut down.

*Despite an intake worker's suggestion that the balladeer makes use of his indoor voice, the reprieve is only momentary. His voice projects louder and prouder. Curled beneath a warm blanket, you try to make yourself as small as possible because in some ways he reminds you of M; whose presence consumed so much space, just the slightest thought of him sucks the air from your lungs and panic beats against your sternum. And you can't help thinking if somehow the space you have lost is directionally proportional to the space M claimed in your life.*

7. American Mountain Ash: *Sorbus americana*
Height: 30 feet (9 metres)
Spread: 20 feet (6 metres)
Sunlight: ⬤ full sun
Hardiness Zone: 2
Description and Observations:
Native to Manitoba, a hardy shrub or small tree that self-seeds quite readily. The bark is greyish brown with upright and spreading branches. A stripped branch smells like cherries. In spring the showy mountain ash produces fragrant white flowers; inviting pollinators. During autumn, bright orange berries gather in clusters and are a food source for wildlife.

❧ You grew a mountain ash from seed in the backyard of what was, at the time, your home on Coralberry Avenue. As the sapling grew, it was transplanted from pot to planter to granite-ringed flower bed. Come spring, the mountain ash burst into flower, filling with air with a spicy scent. Bees buzzed, gathering nectar, pollinating flowers that transformed into ripe clusters of orange berries that offered a food source to squirrels and birds alike. Each year the tree grew with wild abandon, providing shade on the south side of the house. After several years it became apparent that it would eventually outgrow the confines of its home.

🍃 A mountain ash is also known as a rowan tree.

*You're back at the CSU after another round of intense divorce proceedings with M. You're triggered into a state of powerlessness. You can't shake the belief that you will never regain your freedom from him, as if free agency, your body, mind, and soul, were commodities to be owned. You're devastated, thinking that you might remain chained to this man until he decides otherwise.*

*Perhaps it was a good thing that you had no idea how difficult life would be after you left M. How, in many ways, it would still feel like you really hadn't escaped at all. How thoughts of him would haunt your waking hours and stalk your dreams at night. You broke his rules — never lie, never leave, and never tell — and he's punishing you for having done so; for having exposed him and for trying to break the ties of traumatic bonding. You will never be free, never be divorced from M without him saying so, which only adds to your feelings of guilt and emotional distress.*

*After another intake meeting and a review of the daily routine — breakfast begins at 7:00 a.m., meds are at 9:00 a.m., Group is at 10:30 a.m., lunch is at noon, individual therapy is at 2:00 p.m., dinner is at 6:00 p.m., snack is at 8:00 p.m., meds are at 9:00 p.m., in bed for 10:00 p.m. — your belongings are searched for any item that could be used for self-harm. Next is a mandatory shower and the exchange of your street clothes for hospital pyjamas and a housecoat. You're shown to a private room where there is a single bed, a desk and chair, a storage locker, and a windowpane covered with a cordless blind. The tiny whiteboard next to the entrance reads your name and Room 12. One plus two equals three. Three is a magical number in fairy tales — just as forests are often enchanted places in the oral tradition. You place your belongings in the storage locker, hoping that one day you'll reclaim your storytelling roots and that all of the negative connotations and condemnations he seeded within your imagination will rot and fall away.*

8. Japanese Tree Lilac: *Syringa reticulata*
Height: 20–25 feet (6–8 metres)
Spread:15–20 feet (5–6 metres)
Sunlight: ◖ full sun
Hardiness Zone: 3–7
Description and Observations:
The Japanese tree lilac carries an ornamental profusion of creamy white flowers. Come spring, their fragrance is attractive to butterflies and hummingbirds. When the petals drop onto the blacktop of an asphalt driveway, it looks like an overlay of lace. Adaptable to various soil conditions, the Japanese tree lilac creates a beautiful display underplanted with sedums and orange daylilies next to your driveway.

🌱 It has been eighteen months since you pulled into your driveway on Coralberry, which is lined with interlocking brick, granite chips, and an assortment of perennials. The Japanese tree lilac next to the driveway had gone to seed and the yard was unkempt. The all-season radial tires that you'd tried for months to collect from M were stacked next to the walkway that led toward the front porch. The curtains on the house were drawn. The gate to the backyard was locked, as he bunkered in what had once been your marital home. Raven came with you, for moral support and to help load the tires into the car. There was a cardboard box sitting on the tire stack, which you left unopened until you returned home. Inside, you discovered an assortment of personal mail — and a couple of mindfulness CDs. Given that you had requested personal items from the house, including one of the two stereo systems, he knew that you had no way of playing the CDs. Not that you wanted to. You were being sent a message: a reminder that he was trying to "therapize" you from afar. You felt sullied and ashamed. You wanted to take a wire brush to your skin and scrub away his lingering presence. Instead, memories flooded, and the emotional distress led to a ten-day stay at the CSU.

*There are nine of you gathered this morning for Group, including one of the CSU counsellors. You sit at the back of the room in case you need to escape. Today's topic is effective communication, which proves triggering. It brings you back to all of M's claims of being an expert conversationalist and his belief that he could teach you how to effectively communicate if only you weren't so stubborn. A woman in Group speaks to the abuse she has experienced in relation to her partner. Her rage rises to the surface, and her body vibrates as she talks. Your attention wanders to a magazine stand with colouring pages, articles, and resource materials, next to a tall bookcase containing board games. You notice a word-search page entitled "The Forest for the Trees," and you can't help but wonder if the universe is either sending you a wake-up call or merely having a good laugh at your expense. When Group is over, you retrieve the photocopied puzzle sheet; it's a third of the way completed, but you take it, not to practise distraction techniques later on, but as a reminder. For years, you couldn't see M for who and what he was. "You have no clue who you're fucking dealing with," he'd often tell you. He was right.*

9a. Apple: *Malus domestica*;
Family: Rosaceae
Height: 20–35 feet (6–11 metres)
Spread: 15–30 feet (5–9 metres)
Sunlight: ⭘ full sun
Hardiness Zone: 3b
Description and Observations:
There are numerous varieties of apple trees suitable for a zone 3 climate. Apple trees prefer a colder climate with seasonal changes. They come in both standard and dwarf sizes. In order to produce fruit, apple trees require a pollinator to cross-pollinate.

🌿 Perhaps the most famous of apple trees is the biblical tree of knowledge, which grew in the Garden of Eden. Both Eve and Adam were banished from paradise for eating the tree's fruit, which many believe to have been a variety of apple.

🌿 In junior high, you sometimes came home from school stressed out from a day of dealing with racist taunts and bullies, and baked an apple crisp. You loved how the kitchen smelled of cinnamon and how, when the crisp was ready, you scooped some, still warm from the oven, into a bowl. Curling up on the sofa with a good book and a dish of apple crisp was a way for you to self-soothe after a particularly challenging day at school.

🌿 Come summer, at the house on Coralberry, apples would fall from the overhanging branches of a neighbour's tree with a *kthud kthud* into your yard.

🌿 "When you were born, you were the apple of everyone's eyes," your mother said. You could never tell whether she was pleased by this or not.

*You're issued a four-hour pass; time to test the waters after two days in the CSU. Even though you're anxious — it's not as if the stressors have gone anywhere — you're looking forward to spending time with your dog, Toby. Forgoing a taxi, you first walk to a restaurant and pick up a house salad with tofu and a slice of apple crisp for dessert. Walking the rest of the way to the main-floor duplex you are currently renting, you try to ignore the perennials that remind you of your garden; a loss that still lingers over you. Instead, you concentrate on the trees, the interiority of a past that feels ever-present trying to find peace and the possibility of a place called home.*

9b. Crabapple: *Malus* "Royalty";
Family: Rosaceae
Height: 20 feet (6 metres)
Spread: 20 feet (6 metres)
Sunlight: ◯ full sun
Zone: 2b
Description and Observations:
The crabapple is the only apple species native to North America. In spring, sweet-smelling crabapple blossoms burst forth with abandon. The fruit is edible and is often used for making jellies.

Your mother called you her "crabapple baby," a name you've hated for as long as you can remember.

During summers, your mother made crabapple jelly. She picked and washed crabapples from the backyard and cooked them down into a thick mash. The air in the kitchen smelled sweet as you spied, from the kitchen window, birds becoming tipsy on overripe crabapples that had fallen to the ground. If the window was foggy with steam, you'd watch your mother pour the completed jelly into sterilized jars that she later preserved with wax, glass lids, and metal sealers.

*Your first time in Group and you're one of seven people, including the counsellor, sitting around a table. The view overlooks the street and the urban park created a few years back, attached to the grounds of a high school: an inner-city oasis surrounded by chain-link fencing and a desert of concrete. Together, you're playing a game of feelings bingo. We roll the dice and they land on emotions such as anger, sadness, joy; simple tasks such as do a silly dance, make a funny face, access a moment of happiness. As the game begins, people are reticent to share memories connected to emotions they'd rather avoid or those sorely lacking from a full repertoire. The counsellor talks about having grown up in British Columbia and the evergreen forests there — about giant cedars and how the roots of ancient trees rally together during heavy rain, how the roots of one become interconnected with those of another. It's together, grounded by community, that people learn to weather storms.*

10. Brandon Pyramidal Cedar: *Thuja occidentalis* "Brandon".
Height: 10–20 feet (3–6 metres)
Spread: 3–4 feet (1–1.25 metres)
Sunlight: ⬤ full sun
Hardiness: Zone: 3
Description and Observations:
Narrow, upright, and pyramidal in shape, the Brandon pyramidal cedar is often used for hedging. Compact and dense in form, it takes well to

pruning. Brandon pyramidal cedars are fast growing, with bright green foliage. To prevent winter browning, it is recommended to wrap the cedars in burlap after the first hard frost.

A 2006 Honda Civic is capable of holding four five-gallon pyramidal cedars.

You planted seven Brandon pyramidal cedars against the front sidewalk on Coralberry Avenue, a fast-growing hedge that acted as a privacy screen when you were separated from H and on your way to becoming divorced. There was a neighbour who lived across the street, a man you and your offspring referred to as Funky Cold Medina. Funky walked up and down the sidewalk, staring into your yard, onto your newly built cedar porch, into the living room and principal bedroom windows. The cedars grew, and he disappeared from view. But you've discovered that it's the wolf pretending to be something he's not that proves the more dangerous.

Your next-door neighbour, referred to by your family as Her Royal Bagness, removed a mature pyramidal cedar from her front yard because it eclipsed her view into your cottage garden, thus interfering with her ability to harass you the moment you stepped outside and into your yard. The harassment began when you switched your exterior paint colour from bland white to gorgeous clay — a shade of brown that she affirmed sucked all the light from her home. Shouting from the sidewalk, HR Bagness said it was illegal to paint houses any colour other than white in our suburban neighbourhood, and that people who wanted to be different should go and live on farms.

Her vitriol and persistence continued. As a compromise she proposed that you just paint the west-facing exterior wall adjacent to her home white, a request that you declined, which only served to intensify her anger. Whenever you were in your front yard, she would sit on her stoop and hurl insults at you. She would walk along the fence line humming and singing just to make her presence known. She tossed Prairie Traveller's Joy vines over the backyard fence, in hopes of them landing into your swimming pool and clogging up your pool filter. But her worst offence was blocking the driver's door to your car, which was parked on the street, with her van, leaving you stuck in the driver's seat until she decided to drive off. Eventually, you had to report her conduct to the police.

You planted three more pyramidal cedars along the property line, abutting Her Royal Bagness's front yard. You hung hag stones on their branches — protective talismans to ward off her vampire-like sucking energy.

M refused to sell your house so you could escape from her relentless abuse. He said, "You don't run away from bullies," which was easier for him to say than for you to have to live with. The day a for-sale sign was stuck in her front yard was a day of rejoicing for you.

You didn't have the chance to say goodbye to your tea house, surrounded by Brandon pyramidal cedars. Sheltering you from storms, both natural and man-made, the gazebo carried the scent of cedar, which intensified in the rain, perfuming the air with the remembrance of old-growth forests. During summer storms, the sound of raindrops magnified as they danced against charcoal shingles, echoed off the uninsulated ceiling. Oversized screened windows caught the breeze, framed the tranquil scene of cedars surrounding the pond, which was graced by a couple of koi fish you christened Bucky and Lulu — the origin of their names a silent reframe of *fuck you*. They thrived, but by summer's end, you had to re-home them. They wouldn't have survived the harsh conditions to come.

Lying on two ottomans that pushed together and served as a daybed, you watched lightning rip the bruised sky as day slid into night. M crawled beneath Marimekko sheets and duvet atop the queen-sized bed with the sculpted iron headboard; tucked inside a midcentury modern tomb embalmed by the artificial chill of air conditioning. Another flight. Another night spent outdoors, sleeping on an uncomfortable daybed. But it was better to listen to the low drone of the pond pump than your litany of faults he had memorized so well. Better to listen to the steady sheet of water that cascaded from the lip of the fountain into the pond below than to hear the sound of his cheerful morning humming and singing while he made coffee as you sat huddled on the living room floor in tears. Better to listen to leaves rustling in the breeze than his latest sermon of how accommodating he was of you and your fucked-upedness, and how caring he was to let you know how you had better change your ways — and quick. The sound of falling water proved a soothing lullaby. A primordial call to mountain streams leading to an elusive someplace called home.

*There is a poster taped to one of the walls in the CSU's hallways. Its title, "Legacy," appears above a photograph of a coniferous forest, the massive trunk of an ancient redwood next to a sapling. Trees flourished in the garden that used to belong to you. But once you ate from the tree of knowledge, you understood that there was no way you could have stayed with him and survived.*

## FOREST FOR THE TREES WORD SEARCH

```
R O N E D I N L M R D J R A O K F O I
E O D O O W S S A B A K E B O I T U B
P G T R P O P L A R M I D I R A B D R
I D F F U S M P E F R L L O D I L S S
N B E L M Y T S M O K P A O R E R U D
U T D C L C F C B E N R O C T I Y O
J E U W S A H I Y O O W H U H M B L D
R E A R M M B S H R N E R F M C E C G
M M D M I O K U J O O P W A A U E T P
E E A E R R P O T M S K D I P C E A
M S O I C E L T A T S N C E L L N A B
I R O L E D O G O P E D A I E L R I O
M E O H O C N S A D L R P E H R O A I
W C P L E O T E K D O O N A N O O W T
L C U I L R A T F O P I B U S O G S H
L A A I R A D E C O P F O N T H T R R
P W A E D O U G L A S F I R C M O I O
```

| | | |
|---|---|---|
| ~~ALDER~~ | COTTONWOOD | MAPLE |
| ~~ASH~~ | ~~DOUGLAS FIR~~ | OAK |
| ~~BASSWOOD~~ | ELM | PINE |
| ~~BEECH~~ | FIR | POPLAR |
| ~~BIRCH~~ | HICKORY | SPRUCE |
| BUTTERNUT | JUNIPER | SYCAMORE |
| CEDAR | MAGNILIA | WILLOW |

**Therapist**

therapisttherapisttherapisttherapisttherapisttherapisttherapist
therapisttherapisttherapisttherapisttherapisttherapisttherapist
therapisttherapisttherapisttherapisttherapisttherapist
therapisttherapisttherapisttherapisttherapisttherapist
therapisttherapisttherapisttherapisttherapisttherapisttherapist
therapisttherapisttherapisttherapisttherapisttherapist
therapisttherapisttherapisttherapisttherapisttherapist
therapisttherapisttherapisttherapisttherapisttherapist
therapisttherapisttherapisttherapisttherapisttherapist
therapisttherapisttherapisttherapisttherapisttherapist
therapisttherapisttherapisttherapisttherapisttherapist
therapisttherapisttherapisttherapisttherapisttherapist
therapisttherapisttherapisttherapisttherapisttherapisttherapisttherapist
therapisttherapisttherapisttherapisttherapisttherapist
therapisttherapisttherapisttherapisttherapisttherapist
therapisttherapisttherapisttherapisttherapisttherapist
therapisttherapisttherapisttherapisttherapisttherapist
therapisttherapisttherapisttherapisttherapisttherapist
therapisttherapisttherapisttherapisttherapisttherapist
therapisttherapisttherapisttherapisttherapisttherapist
therapisttherapisttherapisttherapisttherapisttherapist
therapisttherapisttherapisttherapisttherapisttherapist
therapisttherapisttherapisttherapisttherapisttherapist
therapisttherapisttherapisttherapisttherapisttherapist
therapisttherapisttherapisttherapisttherapisttherapist
therapisttherapisttherapisttherapisttherapisttherapist
therapisttherapisttherapisttherapisttherapisttherapist
therapisttherapisttherapisttherapisttherapisttherapist
therapisttherapisttherapisttherapisttherapisttherapist
therapisttherapisttherapisttherapisttherapisttherapist
therapisttherapisttherapisttherapisttherapisttherapisttherapisttherapist

## Revolving Doors

If one were to give an account of all the doors one
has closed and opened, of all the doors one would
like to re-open, one would have to tell the story
of one's entire life.

— Gaston Bachelard, *The Poetics of Space*

**McMillan Avenue:**

 The back seat of your car is crammed with cleaning supplies as well as the disassembled metal frame to the gazebo you never had the opportunity to put together while you lived on Telfer Street. You're sitting in the driver's seat, next to boxes of miscellaneous housewares, watching episodes of *Broad City* on your iPhone, having locked yourself out of the main-floor duplex you've just moved into. The key is inside the house. Along with your dog. Along with your things piled inside of one thousand square feet of living space. The sliding patio doors are locked from the inside, barred for extra security with two-by-fours cut to fit the door jamb. There is no way in — just like it feels that there is no way out of this mess.

### Washington Avenue:

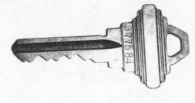 Your father never had to worry about keeping a key squirrelled away under an outdoor mat, because your mother took him and his gym bag back every time; not that he was going to the gym when he left the house, although you suppose some of the women he had affairs with might have been athletically inclined. Even though you were your mother's confidante by the age of five, it's hard to know all the details.

One day during the summer you turned twelve, your father took your brothers out for ice cream at McDonald's while your mother sat you down at the kitchen table to break the news that your father was leaving the family and your parents were getting a divorce. Your mother wept as if someone had died. You didn't understand her tears, why she cared for someone who hurt her as much as your father did. "You have to talk to him," your mother said. "You're the only one who can convince him to stay."

Your mother was kidding herself if she thought you had that kind of power anymore. Turning twelve that summer, you knew that your influence with your father had started to wane. You knew that you were becoming too old for him to care.

Your father dropped your brothers off at home. They ran upstairs, to their shared bedroom, to deal with the aftermath. As your father stood in the kitchen doorway, preparing to leave, you jumped from the living room sofa, ran toward him, and held on with a vice grip. Tears streamed down your cheeks. You felt like you couldn't breathe as you begged him not to leave you, not to abandon you to your mother. Your father smiled, the oddest smile, as if he had just won some game that you didn't know was being played. On that day, you swore to yourself that you would never cry again — never allow someone to use your tears for their benefit.

## McMillan Avenue:

Thank goodness, this is not your landlord's weekend with his daughter. He is a dedicated dad, and you doubt he would have swung by this late to drop off a key had his three-year-old been staying with him. When you finally summon the courage and text him, he promptly texts back that he is visiting friends, or was it his family? Sometimes it is hard to hold on to details, especially when it's past 10:00 p.m. and there is snow on the ground and, baby, it's cold outside. You're in tears, trying to remember that this is not the universe personally trying to fuck with you, but merely a matter of brain-matter overload. You forgot your key inside the rental home, and in the great grand scheme of things this is not the end of the world — it just feels that way.

## Cathedral Avenue:

On Sundays during your childhood, your parents would load you and your brothers into the car for a leisurely family drive followed by dinner at your paternal grandparents' house. Your grandma Daisy would greet you at the back door by swinging it wide open and ushering you inside with a "Come in. Come in," and a "Hello there, my kiddo madoo."

As you huddled in the doorway, the aromas of home cooking greeted you, as well: your grandma's famous fried chicken warming in the oven; black-eyed peas, candied yams, mashed potatoes, and gravy simmering in separate pots on top of hot coiled elements. But it was the scent of Lysol disinfectant — strong enough to make your nostrils sting and eyes water — that permeated the air above all else; your grandmother trying to scrub away stains that only she could see.

As everyone squeezed around the kitchen table for Sunday dinner, your grandmother, ever the storyteller, would share stories of what her life had been like growing up in Truro, Nova Scotia, as a Black child. "When the riot happened," Grandma Daisy said as she piled your plates with food, "the white men came after all us Coloured folks with guns. The adults hid us children in outhouses just to make sure that we were out of harm's way."

According to folklore, a vampire cannot enter a living person's home without a personal invitation.

### Coralberry Avenue:

When you left your second husband, it had been a spur-of-the-moment decision. Your mother had said H was only using you, that he didn't care about you, so you married him to prove her wrong. You knew before you became pregnant with your third child that being with H was a bad idea. You knew before he made one of your daughters kill a field mouse — one she had captured with a no-kill trap and wanted to keep for a pet — with a rock. You knew before he left bruises on your arm and refused to let go of you during an argument. You knew before the name-calling. You knew before he said that the baby was trying to manipulate him with her crying. You knew before he began his hermitage into a darkened mood within the dimly lit rec room in your basement. You knew before he sat mesmerized in front of the television, watching the O.J. Simpson trial for hours on end.

When you told M that you were afraid of your husband, H, he said that you should listen to that fear, that your gut instincts were trying to tell you something. And so, you did. One night in the beginning of March, you snapped to the decision to leave H during an argument over a carton of cigarettes. An argument which wasn't really about cigarettes but about his insistence that you were responsible for everything and he bore responsibility for nothing.

H stormed out of the house and drove to rehearsal. As soon as he left, you told your two older daughters, by now in high school and middle school, to pack up a few belongings because you were finally getting away from him. You threw a few things for yourself and the baby into an overnight bag with as much haste as possible. You were afraid that he would come home and discover you packing. You'd made it as far as the foyer when he came in through the door. He looked at you but didn't say anything. With the girls standing in wait behind you, baby on your hip, backpacks and suitcases at the ready on the floor, you told him that you were just taking the kids out for coffee — a ridiculous excuse, you knew, but you weren't thinking clearly. Fear will do that to a person. H looked at you. He looked at the backpacks and suitcases on the floor. He didn't say a word as he stepped aside, and you and your children left the marital home.

## Washington Avenue:

As a child, you couldn't fall asleep at night unless the accordion door to your bedroom was wide open and the lights were left on in the hallway.

### Coralberry Avenue:

Victoria Day weekend and your mother was camped out on your driveway in her red Ford Escort, waiting for your eldest daughter, Beth, who was going over to her place for a visit. You were estranged from the woman who had birthed you, and she knew that she was expected to park on the street and not on your driveway. It was an attempt on your part to set boundaries while still allowing two of your daughters to maintain a relationship with their grandmother.

You're not sure what possessed you, but you marched out your front door, across the porch, down the steps — heart pounding — to stand beside her car. Your mother rolled down her window, a smug look on her face, as if she was expecting an apology, a *please forgive me for being such a horrible daughter.* Instead of seeking her pardon, you reminded her that she wasn't welcome to park on your driveway and would she, please, park on the street. You don't remember what she said in response. You don't remember what you said in return, save this: "You knew what was going on, and you did nothing to stop it." She was vibrating. You were vibrating. And then she said, "Nothing happened. And if something did happen, I don't remember." You walked away, thinking nothing would ever change between you.

Back inside the house, you removed your flip-flops. You called out to Beth to get a move on from her bedroom. The next thing you knew, your front door was flung wide open as your mother barged into your home screaming at you: levelling accusations about what an ungrateful child you had become, that nothing happened, and, and, and. You didn't want this drama — since leaving H, you had declared your bungalow an abuse-free zone. You said, told, shouted, that if she didn't go, you would call the police to have her physically removed for trespassing. Still she continued her tirade of nothing happened, and if something did happen, she didn't remember.

You don't think you would have actually involved the authorities since you are averse to the idea of your mother being arrested. You'll never know if you would have made that phone call, because by then your eldest daughter had come upstairs with her backpack. Emotionally crushed, you stood aside and let your daughter pass, your mother right behind her.

**Coralberry Avenue:**

M moved in a few years after H moved out. Your middle daughter, Raven, said, "It's like one day this guy just showed up on our doorstep and moved in with all of his stuff."

**Coralberry Avenue:**

M was waiting for you outside in the Honda Civic. You were supposed to drive him to work now that you were down to one family vehicle, and you were also to pick him up after work at 7:30 p.m. — sharp. No excuses, no being late, no being so disrespectful that you would leave him waiting in vain in the lobby of the office building where he worked counselling individuals on the keys to living better lives.

You couldn't find your car keys, your key chain with the half-dozen keys and the Harry Potter souvenir from Disneyland, your grandmother's Las Vegas bottle opener, your grandfather's oblong copper disc inscribed with the Lord's Prayer. You searched the kitchen countertops, the dining room table piled with his files and paperwork, the downstairs craft room with the Ikea pullout futon where you slept at night with the door closed, and sometimes blocked with a dresser, along with a chair, a box, and a bin, because the door didn't have a lock. It wasn't under the pile of blankets or the pillows. It wasn't on your makeshift craft table made from a pair of old closet doors, blanketed with books and vintage finds, and with your Singer sewing machine. It wasn't in your purse, which you had gone through twice. You were wandering room to room in a panic, trying to remember where you had left them, when outside the music playing on the car's stereo system faded, and the hum of the Honda's engine became steely silent, and the car door slammed. It wasn't in your coat pockets as heavy footsteps walked up the wooden stairs, onto the cedar porch, to stand in front of the door — a cottage banger painted hot pink with hinges that groaned, like now, as the screen door opened and M's key entered the door lock, and you knew that your time had run out.

Ever walk purposefully from one room into another, a specific task in mind, only to forget it as soon as you've entered the next room? According to memory experiments, walking through a doorway into another room often leads to forgetfulness about whatever endeavour we were about to pursue. Entering and exiting a doorway creates distinct boundaries which our brains attach to specific activities. This forgetfulness is known as the doorway effect.

**Rapid City, South Dakota:**

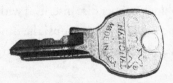

Staying at a cabin resort in the Black Hills of South Dakota, you, M, and your youngest daughter, Annabella, went out for a late supper. The restaurant was outside of Rapid City and, according to him, had an excellent rating on Tripadvisor. To you, a prairie girl, the Black Hills looked more like mountains than molehills as he drove the winding stretch of road to the restaurant. He ordered a pre-dinner drink. Followed by a bottle of wine with dinner. And another bottle. And one more after that. Not being much of a drinker, you were done after two glasses of wine, which you tried to stretch out so it would appear you were keeping up with his alcohol consumption. But you weren't fooling anyone by the time that third bottle came around. He became angry because you didn't want to have another drink. He said, "Well, that was a waste of money," and asked the waitress for the cheque. You didn't want to get in the car with him. You didn't want your eight-year-old daughter in that car. But he frightened you when he was angry, and you wound up with him drunk behind the steering wheel, driving stick because you had never learned, his anger fuelling the speeding engine through the darkness of a South Dakota summer's night. You were terrified that if you said anything it would only make things worse. The relief you felt when you reached the cabin intact and opened the passenger door and removed Annabella from the back seat was palpable.

The next morning, he apologized and promised that it would never happen again. He would never drink and drive, putting all of you and other people at risk. And you believed him. You believed him until you couldn't any longer.

Answer: It happened on three occasions. The time you went out for lunch at a steakhouse and he became angry knowing that you'd had a thing for bad boys in your past. The time the two of you went out for dinner at a French restaurant and he became incensed when you didn't want to drink more than a single glass of wine. The time you went out for dinner for your anniversary and he became infuriated when you suggested he was drinking too much to drive home.

Question: How many times did you open your passenger door to exit a moving vehicle while M was behind the steering wheel?

### Coralberry Avenue:

There was a TV series called *The Dick Van Dyke Show* on in the sixties. The main character, Rob Petrie, was the stereotypical sixties husband — the breadwinner who expected dinner on the table after a hard day at work. His wife, Laura, was his occasionally ditzy but perpetually cheerful sidekick, impeccably groomed in her white button-down shirt, black pedal pushers, and ballet flats. M always had this fantasy of playing Dick Van Dyke in the suburbs. Cast in the role of the traditional housewife, you were expected to greet him at the door with a kiss and a cheerful "Hello" and "How was your day at work?" Fantasy bonus points for having a pot roast warming in the oven and arriving at the front door with a martini in hand, wearing a smile and an apron and not much else.

You have nightmares in which you are standing in front of a doorway. You know that you have to open the door and cross over the threshold if you're going to understand what is

happening, but you're too afraid to even touch the doorknob —
certain destruction lies in wait for you on the other side.

**Hector Avenue:**

You left M after weeks of safety planning with
your domestic-abuse counsellor, Donna. Unable
to make use of supportive housing because of
your ninety-five-pound dog, you had rented a six-
hundred-square-foot house on Hector Avenue on
a month-to-month lease. After dropping M off at
work, you had only a few hours with Raven and
Annabella to gather some belongings in a tiny
U-Haul truck. Before driving off, you tacked a
note on the framed print that hung on the wall
across from the front door in the foyer. The brief
letter let him know that you had left, because you
didn't want M to mistake you for a missing person and call the
police.

> *I'm sorry that I could not leave message that I'm
> not picking u up. But your office was closed. I can
> no longer be with you. It's too abusive and because
> of that I could not talk to you about leaving because
> I am afraid of you & I need to be safe. Don't try
> to contact me or the girls, I will be in touch with
> further details via my lawyer. P.S. I picked up your
> meds. They're on your desk.*

When you arrived at Hector Avenue, you opened the front door
that led directly into a tiny living room, knowing he'd never forgive you.

**Telfer Street South:**

You weren't at home when the two police officers kicked open the side door to the tiny bungalow you started renting on Telfer Street. "It was a last resort," the officer told you as you sat in the back seat of their police car after being located at a park a few blocks from home. "We knocked on the doors and looked through the windows but didn't see any movement or signs of life."

You understood last resorts, yours the kind of desperation that could kick in when your emotional pain became unbearable. Like now. Like the day before when you'd gone by the marital home to retrieve the all-season radial tires and discovered M had stacked them on the driveway along with a cardboard box containing letters that hadn't been redirected by Canada Post and a personal message: a set of mindfulness CDs. A reminder of his therapeutic expertise and his belief that he knew what was best for you because, in his mind, you were the one who was in need of serious help — meaning *his* help — if only you stopped this nonsense and returned home.

You couldn't help thinking that you should have left the doors unlocked. But how were you to remember to do that when you fled the house midway through the crisis phone call with the domestic-abuse support line, afraid the support worker was serious about sending out the police to do a welfare check?

You don't think that you wanted to die. If you did, truth be told, you would have stayed in your relationship and let him put you out of your misery.

**Washington Avenue:**

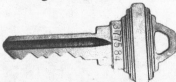

Growing up, you don't recall your parents locking the back door when you retired for the evening. It wasn't part of your nightly ritual. It didn't seem to be a part of anyone's routine in the neighbourhood that you grew up in, although it's not like you went door to door around midnight testing every lock.

**Telfer Street South:**

How to fix a damaged exterior door:
- Supplies
- Wood putty
- Sandpaper
- Putty knife
- Tiny saw
- Gorilla Glue to repair the door lock
- Cream-coloured paint to match the wooden door frame
- Paintbrush
- Bottle of wine for the neighbours

Please note: Keep your receipts as well as the police incident report number for your expenses to be reimbursed by the city. Although, when you leave the Crisis Stabilization Unit, you'll be too embarrassed and ashamed to forward your bills from the hardware store. You will, however, be proud that you have acquired sufficient skill to repair your busted lock and door frame. You make a promise not to act so impulsively next time the past triggers you. Best to leave the door unlocked, better yet a key under the mat, if in the future you feel the need to run.

You have dreams in which you can walk through the doorway into anyone's home, a veritable Goldilocks, wandering curious through people's lives.

**Coralberry Avenue:**

When you opened the front door, it was the smell that hit you — the claustrophobic scent of despair and decay. Two years had passed since you'd been inside your home, the house you had to leave with an escape plan. M left you with six days, exactly 144 hours, to pack up 2,600 square feet of household contents and memories, to prepare the house for the new owners. You brought the dog with you for protection and companionship as the clock struck midnight and you finally had sole legal access and assurances that he had vacated the property. You told your daughters that you wouldn't stay if you felt unsafe, if there was an intruder or overwhelming intrusive thoughts that would lead you down a self-destructive path to no place good.

You went through every room, ignoring the messages he left behind like spoor: his books on Paris; the teddy bear and pink and white gorilla he had given to you early on in your relationship; the women's lingerie in your dresser drawer that did not belong to you. You opened and closed every door searching for intruders, which you now suppose was not necessarily the best of ideas.

When one door closes, another one opens.

**Bannatyne Avenue:**

You are late. Again. Now you are left with the decision to skip Group altogether or do the apologetic knock on the door and mumble your apologies when one of the group leaders comes to answer the door. You knock. The door is opened for you and, sheepishly, avoiding eye contact, you make your way to an empty chair at the table. It is perhaps your fourth or fifth week in Group, in a program designed to help people dealing with trauma. There are eight of you altogether, not counting the nurse therapist and the psychiatrist. You wear a necklace given to you by Beth as a gift after her wedding to Jason. A Giving Key necklace handmade by a company that helps people who are experiencing homelessness to transition into the workforce. Stamped onto the key she selected for you is the word *strength*. You wear the necklace as a reminder, a talisman that, breath by breath, one day M will become less a part of your present and more a part of your past. A woman across the table says how much she likes your necklace. She has one very similar, a gift in support of domestic-abuse survivors.

Once a week, your group begins with a five-minute mindfulness activity, a responsibility shared between members. You find the exercise challenging at times, especially the meditations, which require you to sit back and relax — eyes closed — and to concentrate on your breathing. So much anxiety is held in your throat and in your sternum that in the beginning you find it difficult to control your anxiety. Still, you try your best, even if it means that you don't completely close your eyes. Next the group does check-in and reviews homework and then begins the introduction of new concepts.

Even though you don't add much to the conversation, you're slowly improving week by week. You make a little more eye contact. Your voice is becoming stronger than a whisper. You're beginning to recognize that when a trigger occurs, there is a moment just before your reaction when you can press pause and try to choose a healthier way to cope. The biggest gift the year-long program offers is the coming together of people, all of whom have been hurt in one fashion or another, who offer encouragement and support — the reminder that you're not the only one and you do not have to try to heal from your trauma in isolation.

**Found Objects**

**FIELD NOTES**

Name of Author: _____

Date: _____

Please note: It is recommended that all information be included, even when it is considered irrelevant. Even when it is considered inconvenient and painful. (Where information is considered inconsequential, include an explanation as to why this is the case.)

## Site Location

Primary site location: The living room of a bungalow in Winnipeg, Manitoba, which is located on Treaty 1 territory — the original lands of Anishinaabeg, Cree, Oji-Cree, Dakota, and Dene Peoples, and homeland of the Métis Nation. Additional location on this site: the walk-in closet of the principal bedroom. Please note: all walls are painted the same sorrowful shade of grey, Benjamin Moore Whitestone. (Detail {1})

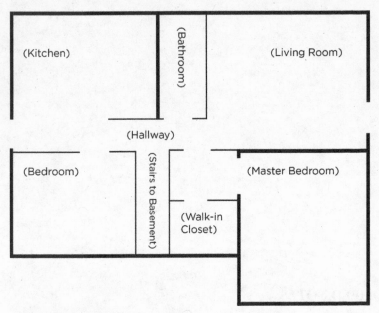

## Additional Site Locations

- The middle table and chair next to the window at the Starbucks on Graham Avenue, where you can order the best chai latte with soy. {2}
- Archaeological dig sites located within the boreal forest of northern Manitoba, along the Rat and Burntwood River systems.
- South Indian Lake base camp.
- The spot along the shoreline where he greeted you after your group docked the canoes.
- The clearing and campfire where everyone gathered in celebration.
- The path he led you down after offering to accompany you to the guest tents because at sixteen you weren't an experienced drinker and wound up pissed to the gills that night.
- The secluded opening in the forest where the two of you stopped and you lost your way.

## Methodology

The deployment of an archaeological field study will prove beneficial by providing distance, a buffer between you and any potential flood of emotions. Years will pass before you are ready to undertake this proposed field study. In the meantime, you will be trying to figure it out — please see Development of Research Design subsection for supplementary information.

Exercise care, as artefacts and memories buried within the sediments of shame and self-blame will be revealed. Keep in mind, the recording and processing of discoveries will be time consuming, and occasionally overwhelming. Employ diversionary tactics as necessary. As the past is reassembled like shards of broken pottery, the following activities may provide distraction:

- Practising restorative yoga
- Walking the dog
- Curling up on the couch with a glass of wine and a blankie
- Watching Netflix
- Searching thrift stores for treasures
- Smashing dishes

Bear in mind, when you're finally ready to undertake this proposed examination, there will be strong, courageous women around you who will offer support, homemade soup, hugs, and guidance.

## Development of Research Design

Exploratory. The examination of the potential relationship between variables, rocks, and hard places, with the state of probabilities including but not limited to the following what ifs: What if your mother had shown you some measure of kindness, instead of constant admonition? "Nobody loves you. If you think someone loves you, you're either kidding yourself, too stupid to know better, or both." What if you hadn't been "Daddy's little girl," and "the apple of everyone's eye"? What if you hadn't been abused in childhood and forced to keep secrets? What if you hadn't been taught that your brown body had little worth or free agency? What if you hadn't been viewed as an exotic other, a temptress, a whore, a scapegoat?

What then? Would that have changed things? Would that have created a seismic shift large enough to have caused you to believe you were not to blame for what happened? Would you have never been so desperate for attention, unable to discern simple flattery from love, unable to hear or heed that little voice inside you screaming danger?

DANGER!

Could he have led you so easily astray, down that destructive path of pine needles and self-reproach? Could you have saved yourself the ruminating on thoughts of *if only*?

If only you hadn't longed for independence at fifteen and signed up for that school trip to Spain, then hired on to that archaeological dig because you needed to pay for the trip yourself. If only you hadn't flirted with him on that long Greyhound bus ride from Winnipeg to Thompson, fallen asleep with your head on his shoulder, said "Let's keep in touch" as the two of you parted ways by motorized canoe to different satellite camps. If only you hadn't waited eagerly to hear his voice on the wireless as you sat in the cook's tent on rainy days, sipping cocoa. If only you hadn't given him such a welcoming hug when the camps gathered at the end of the summer for a bacchanalian celebration. If only you hadn't sat beside him at the campfire and laughed at his jokes, drank all that beer, let him rescue you from that married middle-aged asshole who was hitting on you. If only you hadn't said yes when he offered to walk you back to your tent because you'd had way too much to drink and needed help to find your way. If only you hadn't worn that blue cotton halter top — the one that left little to the imagination — and those low-slung cut-offs, embroidered with flowers, which showed your bare midriff and barely clung to your hips {3}. If only you hadn't followed him into that secluded opening in the woods.

If only.

If only.

If only you hadn't blamed yourself for thinking false bravado should have offered safety.

It will be imperative to consider the validity of empirical generalizations and excuses — the cross-cultural, cross-your-heart, your-cross-to-bear comparisons — such as, but again not limited to the following: *She was asking for it by the way she walked, dressed, talked; by what she said or didn't say,* and *Her "no" meant "yes," despite how many times she cried out.*

In addition, given the inherent temporal design flaws of this field study, you will employ certain repetitive behaviours as a means to supplement and expand your understanding. You will be sexually promiscuous with teenage boys who do not care about you. You will excuse men who mistreat and objectify you and view your fuckability through the postcolonial lens of exotic otherness.

## Historical Research Considerations

Be mindful of contextual factors.

Consider Contextual Factor A: You know what it is to have your language, your heritage, and the names of your ancestors and ancestral homelands taken from you. You're familiar with that untethered feeling that comes from being rootless, of having your Euro-Canadian matrilineal line deny you membership because of the colour of your skin, of having no way to trace those long-forgotten patrilineal ties back to Africa. That knowledge was taken from you, generations ago, just as your foremothers and fathers were kidnapped and sold into slavery.

And Contextual Factor B: You hail from a family of secret-keepers who've taught you well.

As well as Contextual Factor C: You have no idea how to interpret causality, except to believe you're at fault.

This interpretation is similar to the assumption one of your best friends in high school made when she told you what had happened to her at that party with the new boyfriend. You tried to console her. Together you brainstormed for solutions. How to disguise your sex under layers of clothing or fat. Best practices for invisibility.

## Interpretation of Contextual Factors

Interpretation of Contextual Factor A: You come from conquered, colonized, and commodified stock.

Interpretation of Contextual Factor B: You knew how to pretend nothing happened, following your mother's lead, her mantra of denial. Perhaps that is why you were so desperate for love, to belong somewhere, anywhere, as long as it wasn't home.

Interpretation of Contextual Factor C: Girls are taught so early in life to assume responsibility for the sexual transgressions and aggressions of others. Perhaps that explains why you accepted and carried his blame, his shame.

## General Information

The Churchill River Diversion Project was built despite protests, pleadings, and without consultation with Indigenous communities. Natural resources were exploited, reserve lands expropriated, the entire South Indian Lake community relocated, all for the sake of a provincial government's desire for hydroelectric power. Diverting the Churchill into the Rat and Burntwood River systems increased the flow of water into the Nelson River, decimating the traditional landscape and livelihoods of the Nisichawayasihk and O-Pipon-Na-Piwin Cree Nations.

For three months you lived and worked in northern Manitoba. It was your first taste of freedom away from family and the familiar. You were transported with your crew to base camp: a canvas village set atop a rocky outcrop, surrounded by black and white spruce wilderness, next to the water's edge. Although the quickest route to the archaeological site was by canoe, you preferred the slow and peaceful trek along the shoreline enveloped by nature.

The dig was staked with twine, partitioned into squares. You turned the soil with dental picks and trowels, sifted the past like powdered sugar through wire mesh, battling time and blackflies because once the hydro project was completed, the land would be submerged beneath tears and the Churchill River.

Pottery shards and projectile points were gently coaxed from Mother Earth; fragments of the past delicately brushed, recorded on graph paper and sealed away.

Sealed by a kiss.

A kiss sealed your fate.

Lonely boys from the hydro project hovered above in helicopters as you sunbathed on beds of lichen, surrounded by *Seventeen* magazines and bottles of Hawaiian Tropic Tanning Oil. They offered you rides in exchange for a kiss. Their need filled the air like a symphony of dragonfly wings in flight. You found their attention confusing but flattering, flattering but unnerving, and were drawn to it all the same.

Your crew boss tried to run interference. With your caramel colouring and raven tresses, he told the lonely boys, "She's fresh off the reserve and doesn't speak a word of English." You didn't know what to do with his ignorance, any more than you did the attention.

Around the campfire and wood stove, friends from Nelson House taught you words in Cree. You tried to adjust your cadence to a language that sounded like beautiful music while you scribbled in a Hilroy notebook:

tânsi — hello

maskwa — bear

Nisichawayasihk — where the three rivers meet

You learned to catch fish and make bannock, kneading lard, flour, sugar, and salt into a dough baked in a cast-iron pan set over a crackling fire. You skinny-dipped in pristine lakes. Exchanged awkward kisses with a boy from Nelson House whose face you still recall, but whose name you no longer remember. Come nightfall, beneath the brilliance of the northern lights, the warmth of a campfire, you listened to visiting Elders as they told stories and Trickster tales.

Many of these details will be fondly remembered. And although your field notes should have been written on site, or soon after leaving the location, given the circumstances, your delay in providing a written record is understandable.

## Site Excavation

Found objects, missing pieces.

| LAYER | OBJECT | SITE LOCATION: CANVAS BACKPACK |
|---|---|---|
| Layer One | Bic lighter | |
| Layer Two | Khaki bug hat | |
| Layer Three | Pack of Craven A menthol cigarettes | |
| Layer Four | Bottle of DEET | |
| Layer Four | Hawaiian Tropic Tanning Oil | |
| Layer Five | *Seventeen* magazine, May issue | |
| Layer Six | *How to Stay Alive in the Woods* | |

## Artefacts: Location and Identification

**Artefact 1:** A book entitled *How to Stay Alive in the Woods.*

**Location:** The bottom of your canvas backpack that you carried up north.

**Identification:** Paperback, purchased and given to you by your father, contents divided into the following sections: Sustenance, Warmth, Orientation, and Safety. A secondary copy found years later at a thrift store and purchased as a lark.

**Artefact 2:** Boom box and an assortment of cassette tapes.

**Location:** Base camp.

**Identification:** Sony brand electronics, Rolling Stones' *Beggars Banquet*, mixed tapes made by your brother and mailed to you in care packages.

**Artefact 3:** A personal letter.

**Location 1:** Discovered within a family parcel delivered to base camp.

**Location 2:** Recently discovered in a cardboard box situated in the northwest quadrant of the walk-in closet of the principal bedroom. The law of superposition, which states that in undisturbed stratigraphic sequences the oldest layer will be at the bottom of the sequence, does not apply in this situation; i.e., the layering — the photographic dreamscapes from the Black Hills of South Dakota, the letter, the real-estate listing for your childhood home, a series of high school yearbooks — would indicate biodisturbance and therefore cannot be an accurate indication as to the sequential order of time.

**Identification:** A handwritten letter from your father, dated July 1 and yellowed with age.

It was great to hear from you last week for we were all worried about you when we didn't hear from you right away. It is not clear ▮ where you are based. Is it at Nelson or at a field camp?

Everything is just as you left Not much has happened. Clifford received an excellent report "B" honours. Miles as usual is into everything. Your mother is trying to adjust to everyone growing up around her. Cathy was by house to bring the rest of your books and report card.

Your marks for the year are as follows. Math B̲ Science C̲ French C̲ Psych A̲ Eng C̲ Geo. B̲ Phs Ed. <u>Incomplete</u> What they mean by incomplete I don't know, for there was no further comment.

I hope you are enjoying your experience. Please remember not to stray too far from famil- iar ███ ground for that country although lovely, is brutally unforgiving where mistakes are conserned, also because of isolation people tend to show not only their best side, but their worst to extremes so watch it.

Everyone enjoys getting your letters, so write often and share your blessings or lack of same.

Love Dad.

You were warned "not to stray too far from familiar ground." That the setting, "although lovely, is brutally unforgiving where mis- takes are concerned." And that isolation brings out the worst ex- tremes in people; "So, watch it."

Their worst to an extreme? Was this your father's warning or per- haps a projection or self-reflection?

**Artefact 4:** A pair of handcrafted moccasins.

**Location:** Nelson House.

**Identification:** Given to you by Mrs. Spence, who welcomed you into her home. Together you sipped Red Rose tea and listened to CBC radio. You watched her fashion soft leather, smelling of wood smoke, into moccasins adorned with hand-beaded wildflowers in shades of crimson, navy, and goldenrod.

**Artefact 5:** A collection of used bottle caps.

**Location:** Discarded next to the campfire at South Indian Lake base camp.

**Identification:** Molson Canadian.

## Interpretation of Artefacts

**Artefact 1:** *How to Stay Alive in the Woods*, while helpful, ignored certain realities such as the confluence of vulnerabilities attached to being sixteen, female, and a person of colour.

**Artefact 2:** "Sympathy for the Devil" played in the background while you played chicken in motorized canoes. That summer was the first time you listened to Queen's "Bohemian Rhapsody." Freddy Mercury sang "Carry on" as if nothing really mattered.

**Artefact 3:** You believed you were responsible for what happened in those woods, with that boy, and should have known better. After all, your father warned you. But sometimes you can't see the forest for the trees.

**Artefact 4:** Isolation can bring out the best in people.

**Artefact 5:** You thought he was funny and cute, with beautiful brown eyes. At nineteen, he could hold his liquor, unlike you. When he offered to walk you back to your tent, you were flattered. You smiled shyly, envisioning a first kiss, when the two of you became "lost" on the way; stopped smiling when his mood changed, and he gripped your arm, and spoke in a voice barely above a whisper: "Do you really think you're safe with me, out here in the middle of nowhere?"

"I'm not afraid of you," you said, trying to be brave.

"Well, you should be."

The forest fractured into a kaleidoscope of ebony, vermilion red, and emerald green as he transformed into a giant. Or … perhaps he stayed the same, and it was you who became smaller; like Alice, unwittingly nibbling hallucinogenic cookies after tumbling down that rabbit hole.

The next day you awoke in pain, shamed, in an unfamiliar tent and sleeping bag with no clue as to how you got there.

You told no one.

Kept your distance from him until your caravan headed back to Notigi.

Back at camp, you no longer wandered the shoreline alone, sensing danger, his presence, in every rustling leaf and creaking tree branch caught in a breeze. Close to camp and familiar faces, you pretended things were fine. However, it was difficult. Almost as difficult as keeping your head above water when you tried drowning your sorrows with booze and went for that "late-night swim."

## Preservation

Important. Especially of the self.

Sometimes acquiescence, in the face of danger, is the only viable option.

After the camps disbanded, you returned to Winnipeg and began grade eleven. Walking on cement hurt your feet. The storyteller's singsong lilt receded from memory. The comforting smells of sweetgrass and wood smoke left you.

Your new attire, all those extra layers of clothing, generated criticism from friends. Still, you clung to those oversized flannel shirts like security blankets and implemented best practices for invisibility.

## Information Sharing

Encouraged, even though the exchange of information has been historically and culturally frowned upon.

## Further Considerations

What traditional archaeology ignores is the importance of place and storytelling as a way to delineate history.

Bradford Angier, the author of *How to Stay Alive in the Woods*, was a backwoods enthusiast and survivalist. Originally an ad-man from Boston, Bradford and his wife, Vena, moved to a rustic log cabin upstream from Hudson's Hope, British Columbia, along the Peace River in 1947. They lived there for many years, off the grid, until the building of the W.A.C. Bennett Dam on the Peace River created the reservoir of Williston Lake.

Like the First Nations communities of South Indian Lake in Manitoba, the Tsay Keh Dene and Kwadacha in British Columbia were forcibly relocated due to the resultant flooding.

Like the Churchill River Diversion Project, the W.A.C. Bennet Dam caused widespread environmental damage. Severe fluctuations of water levels dislocated entire Indigenous communities; led to the loss of hereditary lands, sacred sites, and traditional ways of life; and negatively impacted fish species as well as native flora and fauna.

Witiko/Wendigo: In Algonquin and Cree Oral Traditions, Witikos are cannibalistic, evil giants. They are supernatural creatures or human beings turned monstrous due to selfishness, gluttony, or cannibalism. The Witiko is towering in size, glazed with ice, or made of ice. Some stories suggest that staring directly at a Witiko will cause paralysis, leaving a person helpless against attack. It is also said that a Witiko will grow in size as it consumes its victim's flesh.

For years, you sensed him lurking in the shadows, waiting to devour you.

## Relevance of Details

**Examination of Detail {1}:** Benjamin Moore Whitestone.
The attribution of sadness is a subjective observation of the subject. Walls do not weep. Although, sometimes they wail.

**Examination of Detail {2}:** Starbuck's venti chai latte.
Please remember that it is crucial to practise self-care and kindness.

**Examination of Detail {3}:** Blue cotton halter top — the one that left little to the imagination — and low-slung cut-offs embroidered with flowers — the ones that revealed bare midriff and barely clung to hips.

Upon analysis, you will discover that what you wore was irrelevant. Similarly, your conduct. His decision to harm you had absolutely nothing to do with you.

## Final Impressions and Interpretations

Pain is like a pebble — a white stone lodged in your shoe. Left unattended, it will cripple you eventually. But remove the stone, undertake critical versus self-critical analysis, and you'll discover the courage and wisdom of that sixteen-year-old girl who survived in those woods.

## Orange

If you are only moved by color relationships, then you miss the point. I'm interested in expressing the big emotions — tragedy, ecstasy, doom.

— Mark Rothko

Colour theory postulates that orange is an energetic colour. Orange is the colour of childhood summers. It's the refreshing citrus taste of orange Popsicles eaten from the back of banana-seat bicycles. It's the cheerful colour of marigolds; of late-evening games of hide-and-seek under the sentinels of streetlights, marking the passage of time before parents start calling out to their children to come inside for the evening.

Orange is a field of Marimekko poppies — palm-sized bursts of joyful optimism set against a backdrop of a bright-white duvet. It's the orange stuffed octopus propped against pillows that offers comfort, its arms coiling around my own. Orange is a Kate Spade old-school tea kettle cheerfully whistling atop the orangey-red coil on the stovetop. It's the orange band circling my favourite coffee mug; a morning ritual of aromatic chai latte as I start my day. I have loved this colour since childhood.

Set against a backdrop of watermelon pink and powder blue, orange is the colour of intense sunsets, like the one M and I watched surrender into the vastness of Lake Winnipeg as we drank wine next to a huge rock blocking out the wind. We talked for hours that night, nestled next to one another, the heat from his body drawing me in like a moth to a flame.

Three days before I left M, with my daughter and dog in tow — a domestic-abuse escape plan safely tucked inside my purse — I drove across town early in the morning to meet the men delivering the brand-new couch to what would become our temporary new home. The couch was midcentury modern in styling, with sleek lines and walnut legs, and was pumpkin spice in hue, purchased from the same store where I'd acquired two much-needed sets of mattresses and box springs.

Orange is part of the colour palette of a famous painting by Mark Rothko. Painted on a large canvas, *Orange, Red, Yellow* displays a series of coloured rectangles that appear to float above the canvas. Chromatic afterimage plays with our perception of colour.

The only perception that mattered in my relationship was M's. He didn't know that I'd purchased this couch; just as he didn't know that I had acquired two queen-sized pillow-top mattresses with matching grey box springs on which my daughter and I would sleep. I would gather enough courage to escape, making true his prediction that I would one day be the one to exit the relationship.

It wasn't that I believed the pumpkin-spice couch colour could make me happy — just hopefully a little less sad and afraid.

As an essential oil in aromatherapy, orange has a calming effect. Studies have suggested that orange essential oil can also be helpful in the treatment of post-traumatic stress disorder.

I quieted my thoughts as the men opened the back of the truck, pulled out the ramp, and began negotiating a pathway over boulevard snowbanks and snow-piled sidewalks.

Orange is the corkboard on the wall next to my dresser. It's plastered with mini posters of positivity, photographs of those who mean the most to me held in place by tiny orange push-pins.

At the open doorway, the men upended the couch; they began a well-rehearsed dance of trying to bring it through the doorway.

They angled it facing east, then setting it south, embracing west, while I shivered in an empty house still heavy with the scent of fresh paint. I silently prayed the couch could be squeezed past that threshold. The men attempted to remove the legs to the couch, only to discover that they were fixed. After hearing the news, I had to excuse myself. I took a moment and sat on my brand-new bed, taking in mindful breaths — *one, two, three, four* — and exhaling — *five, four, three, two, one* — trying to compose myself and quiet the thought that I might have made the costly emotional mistake of leaving M, never mind purchasing a couch that seemed unable to pass through the doorway.

Lucille Ball was known best for two things: the *I Love Lucy* show and her hair. An actress from the 1930s through to the '80s, Lucille had a comedy show on television that she co-produced with her husband. A natural brunette, she decided early in her career to take the advice of her hairdresser, a man by the name of Sydney Guilaroff, who told Lucille that her soul was too fiery for her to be a brunette. She agreed to the change, an apricot colour with attitude. The formulation of the hair dye was so secretly guarded that it was supposedly kept secured in a safe.

Whenever he belittled me to tears, M mocked my cries, characterizing my pain as "wah wah wah, Lucille Ball bawling."

Orange is the colour of the wool coat a young woman is wearing as she walks down a sidewalk bordered by boulevard elm and maple trees. It's the colour of fall, of a harvest moon courting our attention. "Shine On, Harvest Moon" was written by Nora Bayes-Norworth and Jack Norworth and first performed in 1908 in the Ziegfeld Follies. Nora and Jack were billed as the happiest married couple of the stage. Five years later they were divorced.

Did you know that the colour of a harvest moon is due to the moon's path across a sky teaming with dust particles? Ashes to ashes and dust to dust.

Orange is the colour of monarch butterflies, the ones that surrounded me as I sat next to my domestic-abuse support worker on a park bench after another round of legal dealings with the ex.

After removing the screen door and gaining a couple of precious inches, the men were able to maneuver the couch through the doorway. They set it in the living room and then returned the screen door to its proper place. Once they had left, I sat on the couch thinking that it was time to go "home," and that if M were to discover what I was doing, I would be in serious trouble.

Did you know that in Australia the monarch butterfly is also known as the wanderer butterfly?

Orange is the optimistic colour of my Sharpie marker, highlighting parts of my text as I write while sitting on my pumpkin-coloured couch. It is the flame of my creativity candle, the one I light to set my intentions before I meditate or mindfully start my day by writing. It is the spark of magic, the muses, the mantra *Creativity is flowing through me.* A reminder that some essential parts of me are still intact and have not been lost despite years of living with an abusive partner.

Orange resides in liminal spaces, neither red nor yellow, but something born of the in-between. According to the artist Wassily Kandinsky, "Orange is red brought nearer to humanity by yellow."

**Hunger Games: A Quiz**

1. If you feed a fever and starve a cold, what should you have done about your eating disorder?
   a. You had no idea. It always seemed a part of you, like a parasitic twin syphoning your self-esteem.
   b. You had some idea but were terrified to commit to change.
   c. Nothing. After all, you were told Black girls don't get eating disorders.
   d. Reach out for help because Black girls do get eating disorders, and there was no way you were going to beat this on your own.
   e. Is this a trick question?
   f. You didn't want to believe that you even had an eating disorder. You were just extremely disciplined and had an abundance of food intolerances, a profound and abiding compassion for all living things except for perhaps yourself, and a minimal appetite.
   g. Who are you trying to kid?
   h. All of the above.

198 **Persephone's Children**

2. Which best describes your reasons for having an eating disorder?
   a. It gave you a semblance of control when life was complete chaos.
   b. It gave you a semblance of power to compensate for being powerless as a child.
   c. It gave you a semblance of safety in a world that did not feel safe.
   d. It gave you a semblance of mastery over your body; a belief that you could bend it to your will, whip it into shape, force your flesh into a package considered more palatable.
   e. It gave you validation within your family and the larger society.
   f. You rationalized that there were far worse ways to abuse your body. At least you didn't misuse drugs or alcohol.
   g. It gave you a way to appease societal and familial pressures and expectations.
   h. You don't want to be difficult, but you'd rather not consider the question any longer.

3. Which best represents your thoughts when you finally summoned the courage to walk through the doors of the eating disorders program?
   a. Turn and run. Run, run as fast as you can. Things weren't as bad as they seemed, you thought as you calculated how many calories you could potentially burn by running.
   b. Things were as bad as they seemed. So, even if you had to force yourself, you were going to march through those doors.
   c. You should have arrived earlier and saved yourself the embarrassment of walking, in full view, in front of everyone seated in a semicircle.

d. Why didn't you try to lose more weight before entering the program?

e. One of these things was not like the other — you were the only woman of colour in the group.

f. You thought of a million other places you'd rather be.

g. Forget those million other places. You needed this group, this program, if you were going to have any hope of getting well.

h. You were terrified that you didn't belong in the program, because then what would you do?

i. You were terrified that you did belong in the program, because then what would you do?

j. You were afraid that making peace with food and with your body would lead to massive weight gain.

k. Losing your eating disorder felt like you were abandoning your best friend.

l. Losing your eating disorder felt like you were ridding yourself of your worst enemy.

m. Your family, so obsessed with surface and appearance, wouldn't accept you if you gained weight.

n. Society, so obsessed with surface and appearance, wouldn't accept you if you gained weight — and you already had one big Black check mark against you.

o. You couldn't imagine life without an eating disorder.

p. All of the above.

q. Some of the above.

4. You find the program and your counsellor to be:

a. Supportive.

b. Helpful.

c. Guided by a feminist perspective.

d. Empowering.

e. Safe.

    f. Some of the above.

    g. None of the above.

    h. All of the above.

5. Which best describes your response when the woman across from you in Group said, "Women of colour have it so much easier. They're okay with their bodies — having bigger bodies. They don't have the same pressure to look a certain way, to be thin. It's harder for white women, all this pressure to be thin."

    a. You pretended you didn't hear the words that had just fallen out of her mouth.

    b. You avoided eye contact; watched the clock tick away until break time, when you made your great escape.

    c. You counted raisins like rosary beads as you silently catalogued your faults, your body's numerous imperfections.

    d. You sucked in your stomach; tried to erase the trace of Africa from your big-gal thighs by squeezing them together; tried to prevent your flesh from spilling over the sides of the chair.

    e. You looked at her and wished you were that thin.

    f. You thought she didn't have a damn clue.

    g. You felt like a failure, a fraud, an outsider, because apparently a restrictive eating disorder was not one size fits all.

    h. You wanted to say something but didn't want to be mistaken as the spokesperson for all women of colour.

    i. You didn't want to become someone's teachable moment.

    j. You didn't want to become a target by speaking up, to be perceived as a rabble-rouser, the embodiment of the angry Black woman stereotype.

    k. You felt like a disappointment, as if on behalf of women of colour, experiencing an eating disorder or not, you should have said something.

l. You wondered how a statement of erasure and privilege could have gone unchallenged by the rest of the group.

m. You thought, *What must it be like to speak from that level of privilege?* To simultaneously presume that she could speak for all women of colour — discounting the historical traumas inflicted on Black women's bodies since the slave trade — while she garnered sympathy for herself.

n. You wondered, *Why is the pain of women of colour so easily dismissed and ignored?*

o. You went completely still, desperate to fade into the background. You wanted to disappear — which, given your prior history and the nature of your eating disorder, seemed rather ironic.

p. You swore you were done with the program, that it was no longer a safe space.

q. All of the above.

r. Some of the above.

s. You would prefer not to think about it.

6. True or false: Fat is not a feeling.

7. True or false: Growing up, when people said, "You have such a pretty face," it wasn't meant as a compliment.

8. True or false: Being Daddy's "special little girl" wasn't that special.

9. True or false: You can't fight Mother Nature; big bones run in the family.

10. True or false: Sticks and stones may break your bones, but names will never hurt you. But names will never *hurt* you? Who came up with that phrase? You're fairly confident

whoever it was had never been on the receiving end of hate speech or been called:

a. Nigger.

b. Nigger-baby.

c. Watermelon bum.

d. Half-breed.

e. Mooooolatto.

f. Slut.

g. All of the above.

11. True or false: You always hated school picture day.

12. Why did you try to make yourself invisible? Why did you want to disappear?

a. Invisibility was safety. Unseen you couldn't be a target for racism.

b. Invisibility was safety. Unseen you couldn't be mistaken for some exotic other.

c. Invisibility was safety. You learned early the vulnerability of Black and brown bodies; as a child, you witnessed un-filtered hatred on the playground, on the nightly news on television. The trauma of understanding that you were not safe in this world — simply because of pigment — is a fear that doesn't leave you. It became a burden you carried, one that couldn't be shed like weight.

d. Invisibility was safety. No one could touch you if you were invisible.

13. Tick all that apply. Have you ever wondered why your mother:

____ Never ate a meal with the family at the dining room table?

____ Seemed to live on cucumber and cottage cheese?

____ Refused to have her picture taken?

____ Stayed with your father despite all his affairs?

____ Blamed you for ruining her life?

____ Put you on one fad diet after another, while telling you that there were children starving in Biafra, China, down the street, so you had better clean off your plate?

____ Doled out diet pills like Communion wafers, long before you entered junior high school?

____ Told you the world would screw you just as soon look at you?

14. After the incident in Group you decided to:

   a. Quit the program and never return.

   b. Take time to process what had happened and deal with your feelings of being saddened, hurt, angry, and scared. Group no longer felt like a safe space and you'd spent the majority of your life feeling unsafe in this world.

   c. Speak with your counsellor in the program and the group leader and explain what those comments meant to you regarding personal experience, the myths surrounding women of colour and eating disorders.

   d. Speak to the group and address your feelings of being minimized, marginalized, erased.

   e. Talk with the woman who made the comments.

   f. Some of the above.

   g. None of the above.

   h. All of the above.

15. Things you wished that woman had understood before speaking out of turn and out of privilege:

   a. Your body was under constant critique. The texture of your hair mattered. The pigment of your skin mattered. The size and shape of your hips, your ass, your thighs, your nose, your waist, your breasts, your upper arms mattered.

    b. When you looked in a mirror, your image was often distorted. You had difficulty seeing yourself as if you were standing in front of a not-so-funhouse mirror at the carnival.

    c. The bathroom scale weighed and measured your worth, and the thought of giving up the scale was enough to trigger a panic attack.

    d. Your first lover called you his Tahiti sweetie. He would go down on you while stroking your belly. He affectionately called it "your little anorexic stomach." He might as well have been saying *I love you*.

    e. Your family worshipped the same impossible Eurocentric standard of beauty.

    f. It was difficult for you to eat a meal in public, to eat with family around the dining table.

    g. You feared fat like a terrified child feared monsters under the bed.

    h. All of the above.

    i. Some of the above.

    j. None of the above.

16. True or false: You were walking through the shopping centre, heading for your vehicle. You were in a hurry and taking a shortcut through one of the mall's department stores, rushing through the racks of women's clothing, when a full-length mirror gave you pause. You didn't recognize your reflection. You stood in front of the mirror and stared at the person looking back at you. You were painfully thin, and this was the first time you recognized the truth and that you had taken things too far. But then the moment passed, and the image was replaced with how you saw yourself the majority of the time — all wiggly, jiggly flesh and at least three times your size.

17. Why did you wage war on your body? Tick all that apply.

___ You're not sure. This is what you're trying to figure out.

___ You lived what you learned.

___ Your body was under constant critique and criticism by your family.

___ Before 1963's March on Washington and Martin Luther King Jr.'s "I Have a Dream" speech, your parents took you to have your portrait done. You sat on a stage while the artist captured your image in oil pastels. Women in cotton dresses and high-heeled shoes, bouffant hair tamed by hairspray, commented on your appearance, your stellar children-should-be-seen-and-not-heard performance, as they stood next to men wearing summer suits and neckties, crewcuts covered by fedoras. You sat there afraid and in silence, body and character up for critique by strangers, while your parents stood off to the side, basking in the warm reception. It was on this day, shortly after your fourth birthday, when you realized how it felt to be an object.

___ Being the product of a mixed-race marriage at a time when that was fairly unheard of, you were expected to bolster the family's image. Good enough wasn't good enough. A perfect family required perfect children.

___ It was easier to count calories than to count the number of times your mother told you not to become some fat slob with your nose stuck in a book.

___ One family day at the beach, while you built sandcastles, a woman strolled by in a bathing suit. Your father laughed. "Just look at that beached whale," he said.

___ When your family acquired a second-hand piano, you were excited by the prospect of learning how to play. You sat on the piano bench, body conforming to the grooved impression left by others. You loved the soft wooden clunk as you lifted the piano lid, the cool feel of ivory beneath your fingertips. One day your mother walked into the living room during practice. "You need to go outside and play," she said. "Your aunts don't want you growing up to be some fat slob sitting at a piano." You were ten.

____ Your father kept a gym bag filled with *Playboy* and *Penthouse* magazines. Women were expected to look a certain way.

____ Throughout childhood, you spent your entire allowance on comic books and junk food. While your parents held screaming matches in the living room, kitchen, bedroom, you held storytime and tea parties in the attic with your younger brothers. You sought solace in cans of rice pudding, Maple Leaf cookies, Old Dutch potato chips and *Grimm's Fairy Tales*.

____ The tent game had nothing to do with the circus.

____ When you were a young girl, your father often took you with him to Eaton's department store. You watched him flirt with pretty women with peachy-cream complexions and tiny waists at the cosmetic counter.

____ You were "Daddy's little girl," and your mother worked hard to keep you that way.

____ Your father had affairs. You knew this because your mother treated you as a confidante, her shoulder to lean on, her crutch; her cross to bear, because if it were not for you, they wouldn't have had to marry in the first place.

____ Big girls don't cry. They binge and starve themselves instead.

____ Your childhood reader offered no reflection of the face you saw in the mirror or of your family at home. There were the sandy-haired twins, John and Janet, and their blond-haired, blue-eyed baby sister, Anne. You didn't see yourself reflected in Miss Roma's Magic Mirror on

*Romper Room.* Pudgy Black girls were not the stuff of fairy-tale princesses.

\_\_\_ Systemic marginalization and erasure are exhausting. Maybe you thought, *If you can't beat them, join them.* Make your self literally disappear.

\_\_\_ Your family's fear that you would become "some fat slob" weighed heavier than any extra pounds you may have carried. They believed without complaint, bought into the reworking of the racial stereotype: Black women as "welfare queens," lazy and licentious, incapable of controlling their appetites, sexual or otherwise.

\_\_\_ You hated junior-high gym class. You cursed the sadist who designed the school's gym uniform, the infamous "greenie" — that one-piece, bloomer-bottomed bane of your middle-school existence. It exaggerated your round ass, your burgeoning breasts, and your child-bearing hips.

\_\_\_ You were considered exotic; developed a body that men noticed whether you wanted them to or not.

\_\_\_ The day after you had your C-section, your father came to visit you in the hospital. The first words out of his mouth were: "Now what? I know a woman who was back at the gym not long after she had her Caesarian."

18. True or false: In high school, you wore a red shell jacket tied around your waist. It operated as an additional cover-up to hide your hips and ass. It never dawned on you, until years later, that the bright-red colour probably attracted more attention to what some of your female friends called your watermelon bum.

19. When you were twenty-four, your mother looked at you in disgust. She said, "You've lost so much weight, your arms are all flabby." You responded by:

a. Saying thank you for her concern.

b. Joining a gym and working out two hours every day — on top of going to university, raising two small children, and working part-time.

c. Smiling at her from across the dining room as you pushed food around on your plate, feeling this rush of power because no one could force you, no one could make you eat.

d. All of the above.

20. This is a long-answer question. You may use both sides of the paper, and take as many breaks as necessary, in providing your response. How much did a history of sexual abuse in childhood contribute to your development of an eating disorder?

_____

_____

_____

_____

_____

_____

_____

_____

_____

_____

_____

_____

_____

_____

_____

_____

21. True or false: You kept a photograph in your wallet from one of those family portraits specials at the Bay. You were twenty-five and your eating disorder was completely out of control. In the portrait your collarbones protrude, your cheeks are hollow, your eyes cloaked with a sadness you were too blind to see. You called it your concentration-camp photograph, and for some reason, to this day, you can't let it go.

22. When your mother passed away, you inherited the portrait, the one of yourself from childhood, fashioned in oil pastels. The portrait hung in your parents' dining room for years, held you hostage to an ideal that did nothing but harm you. You chose to:
    a. Talk about your grief in Group.
    b. Talk about your grief with your counsellor because Black girls do get eating disorders, and, baby girl, you can't tame that beast on your own.

## Bait and Switch

It is a peculiar sensation, this double-conscious-
ness, this sense of always looking at one's self
through the eyes of others.

— W.E.B. Du Bois, *The Souls of Black Folk*

Portrayed as a gambling game of chance, the shell game is almost always a trick used to perpetrate fraud. Also known as three shells and a pea, it is considered a short con — easy to carry out and quick to perform. The game is played using three or more shells, or containers, placed face down on a hard surface with a pea or small ball secured beneath one of the shells. The shells are then quickly shuffled and reshuffled to confuse players as to the pea's location. As a con, the game's grifter employs sleight of hand to remove and reintroduce the small object. There is no way to win the game.

Born prematurely, I spent my first days of life behind the glass of an incubator, a tiny, café-au-lait curiosity with a straight crop of dark hair. While I struggled for breath, my family collectively flipped a coin and held their own. They wondered if I'd live, and if I did, which side of the coin — heads/tails, maternal/paternal, white/Black — my racial ambiguity would land on.

A pearl is formed due to an irritant inside the oyster's shell. In nature, a black pearl is formed by a white pearl oyster if it has black colouring in its nacre, which is also known as mother-of-pearl, the secretions within the inner shell that provide the pearl with its colouring.

The linchpin of a grifter's con is always a compelling story. A con artist weaves a tale that convinces their victims to have confidence and trust in them. Magical thinking and a less than perfect life make the mark more vulnerable to fall under a grifter's spell.

Like one of my brothers, I had a complexion that ranged from a sallow Mediterranean olive in winter to sun-kissed bronze come summer. Our skin tone's lack of commitment was a source of pride to my father and some of his family. No one considered why they tied our worth to a Eurocentric standard of beauty. No one thought of history, the legacy of slavery and Jim Crow, the internalization of a racial construct lacking any biological basis, a mythology that placed such a premium on whiteness.

My maternal grandmother, Frances, liked to spend time in Las Vegas. Until I became an adult, I thought it was because she enjoyed the casinos for their all-you-can-eat buffets.

The black-lipped pearl oyster, *Pinctada margaritifera*, secretes a mother-of-pearl substance ranging in colour from slate grey to black. It should be noted that the oyster producing the Tahitian black pearl is seldom truly deep black, but rather shades from dark grey to beige to deep purple.

There are six stages to a confidence game: the foundation work, the approach, the build-up, the initial payoff, the hurrah, and the in-and-in. During the foundation work, a short or long con is chosen, and all necessary materials, including backstory and accomplices, are gathered to pull off the job.

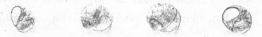

I've often wondered how much of my family's collective past had lodged deep in my DNA like a piece of grit, a grain of sand, an opportunistic parasite requiring layer upon layer of protective scar tissue.

The black-lipped pearl oyster is the oyster of choice for making a cultured Tahitian black pearl. Cultured pearls are harvested by pearl farmers after intentionally implanting a round shell bead within the soft tissue mantle of the oyster. In reaction to the irritant, the oyster secretes nacre, which coats the bead. The more layers of nacre, the higher the cultured pearl's value.

In a confidence game, during the approach (also known as the put-up), a victim is chosen and contact is initiated.

When I was growing up, Grandma Frances often journeyed from California to stay with my family during the summer. She'd claim my room by tossing her suitcases on top of my bed. Within my grandmother's luggage were trinkets squirrelled away beneath layers of cotton blouses and polyester slacks. There I would discover treasures such as Mickey Mouse memorabilia, strands of fake pearls and rhinestone costume jewelry, snow globes from Hoover Dam, lucky coins, and key chains from Las Vegas, as well as citrus fruit from her backyard in North Hollywood, California. But in truth, these pieces of bric-a-brac meant little to me, and sometimes it's hard to turn life's lemons into lemonade. What I truly wanted was to visit my grandparents in the States; what I wanted was to meet my cousins, who were white and lived next door to my grandparents with my aunt and uncle.

One in ten thousand: the odds of finding a white pearl oyster with black colouring in its nacre.

I've often wondered if Grandma Frances and Grandpa Mike ever contemplated the odds of having two out of their three daughters marry Black men during the mid- to late fifties.

During the build-up, the victim — more commonly known as the mark — is drawn into the con by promises of making a profit. At this stage, the ruse encourages the victim's desires to overrule their better judgment.

*Imitation of Life* was a 1959 melodrama that, years later, became late-night TV fodder. Full of racial stereotypes, it was a prime example of the "tragic mulatto" trope. In my teens, I watched this late-night rerun unfold with a mixture of horror, shame, and fascination. My heart ached for Sarah Jane, destined for misery because she refused to accept "her place." I watched young Sarah Jane as classmates ridiculed her, then when, as a teenager, she fell in love with her first boyfriend, who happened to be white — and who later beat her after discovering she was Black. Spellbound, I watched her run away from home and, with few options available, become a burlesque dancer in seedy nightclubs — *white patrons only*. In the end, maltreated and defeated, Sarah Jane retreated home only to discover that her mother had died from grief due to her absence.

*Imitation of Life* informed my worth when it came to dating. I swallowed the con whole: the narrative that I was less than because of my ethnicity. I didn't date often as a teenager, and the boys that I did date were white — my neighbourhood provided no other options. I was always nervous at the idea of meeting a new boyfriend's parents, the uncertainty of never knowing how they would perceive the skin I was in. I was fearful of being seen, not as a person but as colour, a racial stereotype. I waited for the roll of the die to cast my fate as an outsider. I was someone who always sided with the odds of being rejected.

Imitation pearls have considerably less value and are often beads made from glass, plastic, ceramic, or shell that is coated with varnish and a pearlescent substance to produce the imitation pearl's lustre.

During the initial payoff, the mark is encouraged to continue with the game by receiving a small payout, thereby increasing the odds of their continued participation in the game.

On many a hot summer's evening, Frances would take me with her to play bingo. Together, we rode an overheated bus for twenty minutes, with beads of sweat clinging to the back of our legs, which were glued against vinyl seats. Once we reached the ornate Ukrainian Catholic Church on Main Street, my grandmother would let me pull the cord to indicate our bus stop. After we'd crossed the busy street, I would chase after my grandmother as she approached the church, entering and descending the worn wooden steps to the smoky church basement. We'd claim our spot, sitting on hard metal chairs tucked beneath long stretches of wooden tables marred with pen marks, cigarette burns, and copper metal ashtrays. Copying my grandmother, I would spread my bingo cards out like a tarot deck. Assorted bingo chips were scattered like coloured confetti between our sets of cards as the bingo caller spun the metal cage round until a Ping-Pong-sized ball popped out.

Grandma Frances sent me Irish Sweepstakes tickets for my birthday. I never won, but I liked the idea that maybe, someday, I might come out ahead of the game.

During the hurrah, a sudden change in circumstances requires the victim to act immediately or lose everything.

For almost three decades, Winnipeg's Monty Hall was the host of the TV game show *Let's Make a Deal.* The original show aired from 1963 to 1976. Contestants dressed in quirky costumes were randomly selected by Hall to participate in the games and made deals in hopes of winning an expensive prize. In one game, traders were allowed to exchange earlier winnings for a mystery prize hidden behind a curtain or concealed inside a box. The final trader of the day had first choice to hold on to their prize or to go for the Big Deal of the Day, which involved offerings behind one of three doors. Players had to choose carefully. They could win big or wind up with a zonk — a gag prize such as a donkey or a llama.

The black-lipped pearl oyster, *Pinctada margaritifera*, can be found in the Indo-Pacific oceans within tropical coral reefs. Its pearl is considered a rare form of natural pearl.

The in-and-in stage requires a co-conspirator to join in the game. Playing the role of an innocent bystander, they appear to have equal skin in the game as the victim.

A thin wall divided the living room from the kitchen, where my aunt and grandmother, both visiting from California, and my mother were seated at a Formica-topped table. Lying on the pull-out couch in the living room, I was attuned to their conversation carrying through the open doorway. A single globe, hung from the kitchen ceiling, cast a full-moon pearly glow against the darkened screen of our family's black-and-white television.

"You're welcome to come with the kids," Grandma Frances said. "But if you come to visit, *he* can't come with you. And you'll have to tell people they're Spanish."

I heard the push back of a chair. Silence. Then I saw my mother's reflection captured on the TV screen as she silently stood over the kitchen sink and washed dishes.

A natural pearl dropped into a glass of wine will dissolve because of the wine's acidity.

In high school, my best friends, the Twins, would invite me over to their house after school. Sitting at the kitchen table, we smoked menthol cigarettes, drank iced tea. Then we made Rice-A-Roni for supper — heavy on the garlic powder. We'd gossip and bemoan our teenage lot in life while playing Rummouli for pennies. One day, the Twins told me that years earlier their father had passed a petition throughout the neighbourhood to try and keep a Black family from moving onto their street — a fact that once revealed, made me feel nervous and cautious around him. He didn't know that I was mixed race, not until one of the Twins told him, long after I had become a staple in their home. I don't know if I won him over or if he just decided to cut his losses.

Bait and switch. Con job. Rip-off. Shell game. Hustle. Flim-flam. Confidence trick. Racket. Sting. Swindle. Skin game.

M likened my three marriages to *Let's Make a Deal*. He called my exes "door number one" and "door number two" and referred to himself as "door number three" — as if living with him was winning the Big Deal of the Day.

During my twenties, instead of buying a pair of warm and practical winter boots, I purchased a pair of cultured-pearl drop earrings in a gold setting.

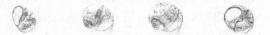

In 2019, I spent a week searching for the ghost of my grandmother in Las Vegas. Frances often travelled there for a weekend of gaming from her home in North Hollywood. As much as I wanted to believe in the possibility of it happening, I came up empty. I was disappointed there wasn't a way to claim that which had been lost. I was frustrated because I couldn't understand why my grandmother would routinely visit a place called "the Mississippi of the West." Initially, Las Vegas had been segregated. The only way a person of colour would have been able to walk into a casino was if they held a menial job there, or were part of a string of Black entertainers who were welcome to perform but unable to stay or spend time in the very casinos that hired them.

In some cultures, black pearls have been regarded as lucky talismans, protecting their owners from negativity. They've also been associated with healing powers, wisdom, and good fortune.

During my childhood, I used to play cups and pennies on the kitchen table with my brothers. There was no sleight of hand involved; just plenty of old pennies and three melamine coffee cups.

I visited Fremont Street and played a single game of slots at the Golden Nugget in honour of Frances. I imagined the ghostly image of my grandmother standing beside the slot machine, willing to answer all the questions I never had the opportunity to ask while she was still alive. I thought that by symbolically retracing her steps I would feel some meaningful connection to my grandmother. Still, all I felt was disillusionment and disappointment — which were merely more of the same. I hoped that I could somehow summon her presence so I could ask her why. Why she chose privilege over two of her daughters and five of her grandchildren. Why she had been secretive about her past. I mistakenly thought that I could hold on to the memory of a woman who had consistently appeared only to disappear from my life.

I don't remember if I pressed any buttons or pulled down a handle, but lights flashed and bells rang and the reels rolled, and that was it. Game over. Downcast, I looked at my daughter Raven and said, "I didn't know that the game had even started."

A pearl's value is based on its appearance. The greater the imperfections, the lower a price the pearl will command.

To have skin in the game, a mark has to have a stake in its outcome.

The top of my left foot carries my first tattoo, an intertwining of a white lotus, a mauve poppy, and a black pearl. I acquired the tattoo months after leaving H, the musician with aspirations of making it big on the West Coast. I chose the lotus as a symbol of something beautiful arising from the muck and mire of intergenerational and personal trauma, the hope that I could transform some of the ugliness of my past into something beautiful. The poppy symbolized a remembrance of strength amidst personal hardship and the pull of family history. The black pearl, the most distinct element of the tattoo, was nestled like a dark moon atop the stamens and pistils of the lotus. I chose the black pearl because I had read someplace that it was unlucky to own one. Unfortunately, M was not a superstitious man.

**Practical Magick**

I grant permission that all might read.

**A Beginner's Grimoire**

## PREMONITION

In August of 2017, I sat across from Sarah, the hospital chaplin, in a private room assigned for family. Halfway down the hall was the neonatal intensive care unit, where my newborn grand-daughter was receiving care. A floor above was the maternal intensive care unit, where my eldest daughter, Beth, spent her first nights after the delivery that almost claimed her life.

**PREMONITION**
The sense that you have dreamt or envisioned something that is about to happen.

"How did you manage?" Sarah said. "Given what was happening in Calgary, how did you do that drive all the way from Winnipeg?"

I didn't tell Sarah about my premonition, the one I'd had a couple of weeks before leaving for Calgary — an image that flashed like a still from a waking nightmare: a crimson operating room, my daughter lying beneath carmine sheets, on a carnelian-red table, blood everywhere. I didn't mention that I'd left despite family and friends saying, "Relax. Beth's not due for weeks. You've got plenty of time."

## WITCH

- A nasty woman.
- An outlier, one who is stubborn and willful; attuned to the seasons, to nature, nurture, the elements, ancestors, and the spirit realm.
- A person historically oppressed by the cis-heteronormative patriarchy.
- A gentle healer, shaman, midwife.
- A woman knowledgeable of herbs.
- A maiden, mother, crone.
- An activist, an ally, a protectress.
- One who believes if it harms none, do as you will.
- One who believes that whatever you send out into the world will return, good or ill, times three.
- A wild woman, self-possessed and self-empowered.
- An untamed goddess, dancing joyously to the beat of her own drum.
- A creator, a crafter.
- One who harvests her own happily-ever-afters.

## IN THE BEGINNING

I was raised Catholic, in accordance with my mother's faith. My father came from a Baptist background, but I have no idea what, if anything, he believed in terms of religion. A spiritual child, I thought of following a religious vocation when I became an adult. But I had many questions that I was not encouraged to ask. I prayed for piety, and for my early formed cynicism to be forgiven. But by the time I was ten, the Catholic Church had lost me. As much as I loved the ritual, I couldn't find a way to reconcile my sense of spirituality, fairness, and justice with the elements of patriarchy, misogyny, and colonialism that permeated the religion.

**Q.**
Q. Why do women and girls have to cover their hair in church, but my brothers, father, and grandfather, all men — amen — don't have to?
Q. If the priests think Mom and Dad's marriage is wrong because of "racial mixing," then doesn't that mean I am a mistake, as well?
Q. How come I can become a nun, but I can't be a priest or the Pope?
Q. Why are the souls of unbaptized babies sent to Limbo?
Q. How come there's a God but not a Goddess?
Q. Why does Eve carry all the blame for getting kicked out of Eden?
Q. Why should women be made to suffer in childbirth?
**A.**
A. Stop asking so many questions. Don't you know children should be seen and not heard?

## FORGIVE ME, FATHER, FOR I HAVE SINNED

As a child, I thought that I had magical powers. Not like Hermione Granger or like Samantha Stephens on *Bewitched* — I couldn't wave a magic wand, say a few magic words, or twitch my nose and *poof*, there was a unicorn juggling dishes in the kitchen. No, mine was a practical magic, lacking in highjinx and general hilarity. I thought I could prevent catastrophes from happening — if I believed hard enough. It was a skill that came in handy because monsters lurked in the musty basement of my childhood home. They roamed the cobwebbed attic while vampires hovered at the threshold to my bedroom, waiting to drain me dry.

Perhaps the belief that I could prevent bad things from happening was my way of dealing with the lack of security and safety I experienced at home: a home in which my parents constantly screamed at one another, and made me their confidante and scapegoat; a home in which my father had affairs, and one foot out the door, and my mother had regrets, and rage and Rx bottles.

## MAGICAL THINKING

- The belief that your thoughts, wishes, and desires directly influence the world around you.
- According to Jean Piaget, in the pre-operational stage of cognitive development, children ages two to seven make use of magical thinking to understand and exercise control over their environment.
- Magical thinking: a mental illness in adults.
- Magical thinking: culturally agreed-upon beliefs lacking scientific basis.

Perhaps it was my way of dealing with the lack of safety I felt in a world in which four little African American girls, preparing for Sunday school, could be murdered in a bomb blast at a Baptist church in Birmingham. Perhaps it was my way of dealing with the nightly news as I witnessed children — captured on camera — being beaten with firehoses, bitten by police attack dogs, cudgelled with police batons, called "nigger" and told "Go back to where you came from," being arrested as they marched for freedom, for segregation to end and for Black lives to matter.

**MAGIC**
A sleight of hand, a performance trick, a source of entertainment, an illusion.

**MAGICK**
A belief system often othered, effecting change by working with the elements of nature, in harmony and with focused attention.

## GOD BLESS THE CHILD

It was 10:22 a.m. when the blast occurred in that church basement down in Birmingham, 10:22 a.m. when ten or more sticks of dynamite were planted near an outside staircase of the 16th Street Baptist Church. They exploded with an intensity that shook the ground and could be heard three blocks away. Pages from song books and the bible floated in the air like autumn leaves and fell to the ground, covered in blood and chunks of concrete and shards of broken glass. All the stained-glass windows were destroyed except for one: Jesus with a group of children, his face blown out. Suffer the little children to come unto me.

## ON RITUAL

- A ritual can be that first cup of coffee in the morning. It can be a prayer, a blessing, a sacrament; the brushstroke of fingertips, the sign of a cross made from forehead to heart, left shoulder to right. A ritual can be the flesh of defrosted cod, coated in cornmeal, fried in a pan, and served with canned green beans, mashed potatoes, and plenty of Our Fathers at Friday dinner. It can be the waft of frankincense and myrrh from the censer. Words spoken by men in a dead language, words imbued with the power to transform wine into blood, bread into flesh. It can be a wafer balanced on the tip of your tongue, a wafer swallowed whole, filling a spiritual hole with purity and goodness.
- A ritual can be a rite of passage, commemorated with family, friends, and community.
- Ritual can be a form of compulsion, a symptom of obsessive-compulsive behaviour.
- Ritual can be the casting of circles and spells, Rootwork and Conjure, the celebration of Sabbats and Esbats, goddesses and nature, the nurturance of all living things, respect for field and forest, mountain and stream, river and ocean, the air you breathe. Ritual can be the remembrance of ancestors, of whom you are and have always been.

Surviving in this white colonial cis-heteropatriarchal society is a form of **BLACK GIRL MAGIC.**

## SIMPLE RITUALS FOR PROTECTION DURING SLEEP

### Freshen Nightly

*Water: Fill a small glass with water and leave next to your bedside table at night. The water will trap negative energy. Never drink this water, and come morning discard outside.*

### Freshen Weekly

*Salt: Lightly sprinkle black or rock salt on your mattress, as well as beneath your pillow.*

*Rosemary: Place a sprig of rosemary in each corner of your bedroom to deter unwelcome spirits.*

Matthew, Mark, Luke, and John,
Bless the bed that I lie on.
If I should die before I wake,
I pray the Lord my soul to take.

I had a nightly bedtime ritual during childhood. I would leap on to the mattress, in hopes of avoiding whatever monsters lurked beneath the bed waiting to grab hold of my ankle. I crafted a protective fort made from scratchy woolen blankets; touched my fingertips to eyelids; prayed and conjured guardian angels, tiny as Tinkerbell, to circle overhead as I slept. I said my prayers before going to sleep. It wasn't lost on me, even as a child, that I was hedging my bets in case I died during the night — a thought that wasn't exactly comforting.

## RABBIT, RABBIT

Rabbit is a spirit guide. It sits motionless, not out of fear but to avoid detection.

Rabbit: a sign of fertility, creativity, abundance, sensitivity, awareness, survival.

It's considered good luck for *rabbit, rabbit* to be the first words out of your mouth on the first day of the month.

## HEY, SILLY RABBIT, TRICKS ARE FOR KIDS

After my brothers and I survived church with our mother, we'd pile into the family car, with my father at the helm and my mother by his side. Sundays meant time for a leisurely drive followed by dinner at his parents'. We lived in a city criss-crossed by rivers and creeks, which meant bridges, which meant holes appearing in the middle of them (cue disaster movie sequence; cue terrifying, crumbling abyss; cue family car teetering on the edge, then plummeting over the precipice, careening into the murky depths, with my family and me trapped inside and drowning).

As a child, I couldn't understand why my parents and brothers were oblivious to the danger. I wondered, was it because my mother and father were too busy fighting, and my brothers too busy ignoring the chaos, that they had no cause for concern? Or was it because they were secure in the knowledge that I would do all that I could to save them? And so I learned to conjure an invisible protective bubble that would envelop the car, transporting me and my family safely to the other side.

## CHILDHOOD FAVOURITES

**Throughout history, independent women have always been accused of witchcraft.**

My mother said that I was a stubborn and willful child.

- Favourite TV show: *Bewitched*
- Favourite movie: *The Wizard of Oz*
- Favourite Disney movie: *The Three Lives of Thomasina*
- Favourite holiday: Halloween
- Favourite book(s): *Grimm's Fairy Tales* and Greek mythology
- Favourite place(s) to be: hidden amongst the peonies, irises, and bleeding hearts that bloomed in my mother's garden; walking next to the creek, amongst the towering oaks in Kildonan Park

As a child, my favourite television show was *Bewitched*. Part of the attraction was that *Bewitched* was the only depiction of a "mixed-race" marriage on television. Granted, the union was between a witch and a mortal — but still. The television show resonated with me as the mixed-race offspring of a Black father and a white mother. Watching the show, I never understood why Samantha tried so hard to conform to Darrin's narrow-minded, patriarchal definition of respectable womanhood: the role of traditional housewife, catering to her husband's every whim and desire. I never understood why she chose to deny her true self, her magick, just to please some man. Every week I kept watching, hoping Samantha would come to her senses, twitch her nose, and blow that pop joint.

## CATHOLIC FOLK MAGIC

The women in my mother's family were a superstitious lot. If a bird flew into the house, it was a harbinger of death. If a mirror broke, count on seven years' bad luck. Our futures, or lack thereof, were divined in the slew of tea leaves swirling on the bottom of delicate teacups. The shapes formed by melting candle wax were a tool for divination. A key suspended from a cord and held over a pregnant woman's belly could reveal the baby's gender based on the pendulum's direction of swing.

Saints were called on and petitioned for all manner of things: to provide safety while driving, heal sickness, help sell property, encourage weight loss, improve Grandma Frances's odds at the casino. None of this was considered incongruent with their Polish Catholic faith.

### Petitioning St. Joseph to Help with the Sale of Your Home
*Supplies needed:*
- *A hand trowel.*
- *A statue of Saint Joseph.*
- *Prayer to petition Saint Joseph.*

*Directions:*
*Dig a hole and bury the statue of Saint Joseph (placed upside down) in your front garden, facing toward your home, and recite the following prayer. If you're unable to do this yourself, ask your real estate agent to oblige because you need your home sold as soon as possible.*

> *O, Saint Joseph, you who taught our Lord the carpenter's trade, and saw to it that he was always properly housed, hear my earnest plea. I want you to help me now as you helped your foster-child Jesus, and as you have helped many others in the matter of housing. I wish to sell this [house/property] quickly, easily, and profitably, and I implore you to grant my wish by bringing me a good buyer, one who is eager, compliant, and honest, and by letting nothing impede the rapid conclusion of the sale.*
>
> *Dear Saint Joseph, I know you would do this for me out of the goodness of your heart and in your*

*own good time, but my need is very great now, and so I must make you hurry on my behalf.*

*Saint Joseph, I am going to place you in a difficult position with your head in darkness, and you will suffer as our Lord suffered until this [house/property] is sold. Then, Saint Joseph, I swear before the Cross and God Almighty, that I will redeem you and you will receive my gratitude and a place of honour in my home.*

*Amen.*

## ROOTWORK

- A practice based on herbs, rocks, stones, and working with the elements of nature and the ancestral spirits to promote healing, cast spells, and solve problems.
- A form of African American folk magic. Also known as Conjure or Hoodoo in the southern United States. *Hoodoo* is derived from the word *Juju*, meaning "magick."

> Grandmothers across an ocean of tears, of blood, in chains, you brought your strength, your courage, and your wisdom.

## LA MADAMA

Traditionally a spirit guide, La Madama provides assistance and advice in times of need and with daily affairs. She is the matriarch of home and hearth, knowledgeable in the ways of herbs and herbal medicine. La Madama is fiercely protective of those she cares for. She is the embodiment of the spirits of female slaves, the old Rootworkers and Conjure Women,* healers and midwives. She carries their wisdom. Treat her with respect and love.

### Instructions to Erect a Shrine to the Spirit Guide La Madama

*Lay a white, orange, or red cloth on a table and place a doll or statue of La Madama on top. Offer a glass of cool water, a vigil candle, and an offering consisting of a deck of cards, strong spirits, tobacco, brown sugar, molasses, cooked rice, home cooked meals, black coffee, healing herbs, and flowers.*

---

* "For its part, Conjure spoke directly to the slaves' perceptions of powerlessness and danger by providing alternative — but largely symbolic — means for addressing suffering. The Conjuring tradition allowed practitioners to defend themselves from harm, to cure their ailments, and to achieve some conceptual measure of control over personal adversity." (Yvonne Chireau, "Conjure and Christianity in the Nineteenth Century: Religious Elements in African American Magic.")

In 1913, *Webster's Unabridged Dictionary* defined *Hoodoo* as:

- ~~n. One who causes bad luck.~~
- ~~Same as voodoo.~~
- ~~Bad luck.~~
- ~~v. t. 1. To be a hoodoo to; to bring bad luck by occult influence; to bewitch.~~

#### #MagicResistance

I've collected Black Americana for years. A strange interest to some. An uncomfortable reminder of history to others. When I find a vintage piece and bring it home, I feel like I am offering respite and sanctuary. Now, I understand why.

## HOW TO DRY HERBS

- *Harvest early in the morning to preserve essential oils.*
- *Snip/pinch stalks.*
- *Tie stems in bundles of no more than twelve.*
- *Hang upside down in a cool, dry place until dry.*

*Note: Do not dry herbs in direct sunlight. If saving seeds or flower heads, place the bundle in a paper bag before hanging upside down.*

## GREEK MYTHOLOGY AND PERSEPHONE

During my childhood and adolescence, I was drawn to reading Greek mythology. There was something about the capricious whims of the Greek pantheon, their concern for mortals coupled by their vindictiveness and petty grievances, that drew me into their stories. I was fascinated by the ruler of the gods, Zeus, and his ongoing infidelities, and by his wife, the goddess Hera, who was furious about his betrayals. Even now I remember the story of Io, a mortal woman Zeus lusted after. Hera transformed her into a heifer in order to keep Zeus from his intended paramour, a woman she further cursed with the constant bite of a gadfly in hopes of driving her mad. I still recall the tale of Narcissus, enamoured by his reflection in a pool of water, who rebuffed the affections of the nymph Echo and was transformed into a flower as punishment. But the story that I was most drawn toward was that of Persephone, the daughter of Zeus and Demeter, the goddess of agriculture and fertility.

According to the mythology, Demeter and Persephone were very close. One day Persephone went for a walk with her maidens but, enchanted by flowers growing in a meadow, she became separated from them. Drawn to a resplendent narcissus, Persephone stooped to pluck the flower. The ground beside her crumbled and Hades, god of the underworld, arose from the depths in his chariot to spirit her away and make her his consort.

Separated from her daughter, Demeter searched the land for Persephone, but to no avail. In her grief, she neglected her duties. Crops failed and people began to starve. When she finally discovered that Zeus had approved of Hades's desire to wed Persephone, Demeter refused to usher in spring until her daughter was returned to her. With famine raging amongst mortals, Zeus tasked the god Hermes to bring his daughter back to the land of the living. However, unbeknownst to all, Hades had encouraged Persephone to eat the seeds from a pomegranate. Having eaten from the food of the dead, Persephone was bound to live with Hades below for six months of the year — one month for every seed consumed. The other six months she was allowed to return to her mother, not as the queen of the underworld, but as the young maiden Kore, goddess of fertility. Demeter welcomed her daughter's return, and her joy at the reunion caused spring to return and crops to grow. When Persephone's time on Earth came to an end and she returned to the underworld, Demeter's sadness caused crops to fail and harsh winter to come until her daughter's return the following springtime.

I often wondered how Persephone managed, having a dual identity as queen of the underworld and as Kore the maiden and goddess of fertility. I wondered how Persephone felt having to perpetually straddle two worlds through no fault of her own. And I marvelled at a mother whose love would drive her to such great lengths to have her daughter returned to her.

## TALISMAN

**TALISMAN**
A magical object providing protection against ill will or the supernatural, or providing assistance such as good luck, good health, or power(s).

I did tell Sarah about the talisman I brought with me, though: the photograph that I'd removed from my refrigerator and tucked on the dash the morning I loaded my luggage and dog, Toby, into the car and headed, west, out of Winnipeg. In the photograph, my daughters were posed in my garden, beside our front porch covered in clematis. They were surrounded by stocks of lamb's ear, delicate sprays of pink astilbe, variegated dogwoods, and a Crimson Frost birch with fairy bells from the last Winter's Solstice hanging from its branches. Over her summer outfit, Beth wore a black choir robe and skinny tie. Annabella, the youngest, was dressed in a black cape over a blue T-shirt and skinny jeans, with Harry Potter–style glasses resting on the bridge of her nose. Raven sported similar eyewear, and a black-and-white-striped scarf was wrapped around her neck. Next to Raven was Jesse, the husky mix she'd rescued as a puppy. Jesse flaunted a purple cape and a black witch's hat. My adult daughters carried smiles on their faces and broomsticks in their hands.

"It's my favourite photograph, of my favourite people, in one of my favourite places," I said to Sarah.

I drew strength from that photograph when, as I sat parked at a gas station in Brandon, my son-in-law's texts started coming: *routine ultrasound … baby's in distress … we're in the ambulance … prepping Beth for emergency c-section.*

I drew courage as I drove the Trans-Canada Highway, understanding that my daughter was in peril. *Baby's here … okay but tiny ... such a cutie ... will send pic shortly ... let her sisters know ... Beth's still in the operating room ... Lost lots of blood cuz of the fibroids but they're taking care of her.*

And I drew determination as I focused on Beth, seven hours on the operating table, and the highway in front of me. *They can't stop Beth's bleeding ... ordering more blood ... they can't stop the bleeding ... doctor says to pray.*

Fifteen hours I drove, straight through to the hospital in Calgary, my fingertips touching that photograph like a talisman as I sent a litany of silent prayers into the universe and tried to project my strength; wanting to imbue my daughter with the will to fight, wanting her to remember that she came from strong stock, and to know that I was on my way.

Vocal Lessons: A Diagnostic Report

| | |
|---|---|
| **Name:** Rowan McCandless | **Date of examination:** Sept. 26, 2015; March 4, 2016; April 1, 2017; July 5, 2018; and May 21, 2019 |
| **Informant:** self-reported | **Tentative Diagnosis:** Expressive Language Deficit, TMJ disorder |
| **Examiner:** SLP | **Referred by:** self-referral |

## STATEMENT OF THE PROBLEM:

Ms. McCandless reports having experienced a long-term abusive relationship, the dynamics of which stifled her creative expression as a writer as well as her actual voice. Additionally, the client notes that she finds it difficult to verbally express herself, especially in conflict situations. Furthermore, the client states that her ex-husband believed she lacked the skill sets required for effective communication.

## OVERVIEW AND OBJECTIVES:

The client will:

- Create new behavioural pathways leading to self-expression.
- Categorize the ways in which she has been encouraged and/or discouraged from using her voice.
- Consider the numerous ways she has been silenced.
- Research techniques to improve vocal quality.
- Reflect on circumstances which have affected verbal communication style.

## BACKGROUND INFORMATION:

Primary Language: English — by default. Although her mother's linguistic background was bilingual (both English and Polish), no attempt was made to pass the Polish language on to the client. Further, she bears no trace of her paternal grandfather's South Carolinian lilt. Additionally, she has lost all trace of Mother Africa from her tongue, an ancestral legacy stripped from intergenerational memory because of the transatlantic slave trade.

## FAMILIAL HISTORY:

Based on questionnaire A17 (attached under separate cover and available upon written request), the client reported the following dictums that were to be followed within her family of origin:

- Children should be seen and not heard.
- We do not air our dirty laundry in public.
- What goes on in this house stays in this house.
- Blood is thicker than water.
- Hear no evil. See no evil. Speak no evil.
- Honour thy father and thy mother.
- If you can't say anything nice, don't say anything at all.

**MARITAL HISTORY:**

The client has been married three times, which may be due, in part, to her family system. She reports that there were numerous marriages and divorces occurring on the paternal side of her extended family.

The client reports having had no issues communicating with her first husband, R. Those problems came later, over child-rearing decisions after their separation and divorce. With her second husband, H, it appears that there were subjects not to be talked about or shared because she was afraid of his anger. She was additionally afraid of H making good on his threat to kill himself if she left him and concerned about the judgment that might come from family and friends if they knew of the abuse happening. It cannot be stressed highly enough that these situations fall under the umbrella of an abusive relationship. It is my belief that she was therefore in a vulnerable state when she met M, who became her third husband. Ms. McCandless states that with M, communication, or the lack thereof, was an ongoing topic of conversation initiated by her ex-partner. There were many subjects she couldn't speak about in his presence, such as her feelings of isolation after he made her cut off contact with friends and family, leaving M the only person she had to confide in. She couldn't talk about the coercion and control — the grief and guilt she carried surrounding the abortion he forced her to have. She couldn't talk about his treatment of her over the years. The only perceptions that were valid, the only opinions that mattered, according to Ms. McCandless, were his. Further, it appears that the quieter she became, the louder he'd become, telling her:

- No matter what, we talk.
- You're so far up your family's ass that you can't hear me.
- Not talking violates everything we are about.
- You always interrupt.
- You always argue.

- It's always about you and your story.
- I could teach you how to communicate if you just let me.

**TERMS:**
Communication: a process by which information is exchanged between individuals through a shared system of symbols, signs, and verbal and non-verbal behaviours.

Active listening, as defined by the client: the ability to sit quietly and offer no feedback unless solicited by M.

**COMPETENCIES AND GOALS:**
It is hoped that the re-examination of the past will lead to the client's understanding of the influences that have affected her voice. Further, the purpose is to help the client restore her voice, to help her communicate in ways that have felt uncomfortable and impossible — to reclaim her power from a situation that had rendered her powerless.

**ARTICULATION:**
Words tripped over the client's tongue — specifically, specificity and, at certain times and with certain people, *I love you*.

**ESSENTIAL QUESTION:**
Is it possible to reclaim one's voice after it has been taken away?

**BODY OF THE REPORT:**
Explore familial and personal histories for commonalities which have impacted the client's verbal and nonverbal communication styles.

**OBSERVATIONS AND ANECDOTAL EVIDENCE:**
The client reports that, when she was four, the family's backyard tandem swing set would transform into a magical coach that

could lead her to places far away from home, her legs straddled, her arm muscles flexed as she pushed the white wooden platform from side to side, faster and faster. According to Ms. McCandless, words began to fall from her mouth like bits of bituminous coal. Snippets of memories of her mother, and father, gathered at her sandalled feet like unwanted offerings. The client states that her mother, standing in the kitchen with the window wide open to catch the summer's breeze, could hear what she was saying. Her mother rushed outside, grabbed young McCandless by the arm, and yanked her from the swing. She led her through the back door, past the kitchen, and into the tiny bathroom with the pedestal sink, where a bar of soap lay in wait. The client recalls that the soap tasted horrible.

Ms. McCandless often had singing competitions with her maternal cousin, Michael, when they were children. After her uncle's jazz band's practice, the family would gather round on sofas and chairs as she and her cousin took turns asking for requests of oldies: "Michael Row the Boat Ashore," "King of the Road." She aspired to win the handful of change collected from pant pockets and shiny black-patent pocketbooks that was awarded to the best performance. She took turns with Michael, belting out tunes loud enough to be heard throughout the main floor of her aunt and uncle's home, where drum kits and guitars took up space in the dining room. This is significant, as it demonstrates that she was able to use her voice effectively and joyously in some situations.

The client's father repeatedly said, "But don't tell your mother."

When she was eight, Ms. McCandless's parents had a concrete patio built in their backyard. It was painted the colour of goldenrod and made a cheerful stage for recounting fairy tales, Saturday morning cartoons, and imaginative skits with her friends. The client states that it was one of the few places in childhood where she could freely express herself. It would appear that creative self-expression was important to the client from an early age. This interest, whether communicated vocally or in some other fashion, is indicative of someone quite capable of conversational turn-taking.

Throughout Ms. McCandless's childhood, her mother would take her aside and vent about her husband's affairs. When she was done releasing her frustration, she would say repeatedly, "But don't tell your brothers." It can be surmised from anecdotal reports that there was, within her family of origin, a concerted effort to enforce secrets and that Ms. McCandless, from an early age, was given the role of family secret-keeper.

In grade five, the client performed a duet with another girl for the school's Christmas pageant. They were to harmonize, but Ms. McCandless kept slipping into the other girl's part, which frustrated their music teacher to no end. Practice after practice didn't change things. She couldn't hear her singing voice separate from another's.

At some point during her adolescence, the client reports reading Dr. Maya Angelou's autobiography *I Know Why the Caged Bird Sings*, in which Dr. Angelou depicted her life from the age of three to sixteen. By way of context, after being buffeted from one family member's home to another, young Maya and her brother are sent by their father to live with their paternal grandmother, a successful store owner in Stamps, Arkansas. Racism permeated Maya's everyday life, affecting her self-esteem. Eventually, Maya and Bailey's father showed up in Stamps. When he departed, he left Maya and her brother in St. Louis, Missouri, with their mother, Vivian, and stepfather, Mr. Freeman, the latter first molesting, then later raping the eight-year-old, Maya. After Maya disclosed the abuse, Mr. Freeman was arrested, but he escaped jail time. Later he was discovered murdered — most likely by people connected to the family. Believing that it was her fault, that her words had caused a man's death, Maya became selectively mute. Through the love of her grandmother and the assistance of a kindly teacher, Mrs.

Bertha Flowers, who encouraged Maya to read and recite book passages, she regained her voice. Similar to Dr. Angelou, books saved Ms. McCandless as a child.

The client reports that one day while she sat in junior high French class, her name was called over the intercom above the dramatic murmurs of classmates. Ms. McCandless asserts that it was very uncharacteristic for her to be called down to the principal's office. She left behind the conjugating of verbs — *je parle, tu parles, il/elle parle, nous parlons, vous parlez, ils/elles parlent* — and walked down a short hallway to the steps that led down to the main-floor office. The secretary, seated at her office desk, let Ms. McCandless know that the school nurse wanted to talk with her. About what, she had no idea as the nurse popped into the office to escort her to the nurse's room. According to the client, the room had an antiseptic smell, and she remembers the nurse asking, "How are things going at home?" The client states that she stood there, trembling as a rigidity rose from her toes toward the top of her head. The client believed that she couldn't speak a word against her family, couldn't breathe a word to what was happening at home. No consideration was given as to how inappropriate it was to give a child such responsibility: the task of keeping the family together and herself, as well as her siblings, out of the foster-care system. She didn't say a word as tears pooled in her eyes. She didn't utter a sound. She kept the secrets safe until, frustrated, the school nurse sent her back to the classroom.

At thirteen, Ms. McCandless belonged to the drama club at her local junior high school. She loved being onstage, where it was encouraged to make use of a good, strong voice. She especially enjoyed playing one of the three witches in *Macbeth*, casting spells and conjuring visions of future events over a cauldron. Ms. McCandless reports that she had no issues with projecting her voice, which subsequently made her wonder why her voice would catch in her throat and come out as a raspy whisper toward the end of her relationship with M. It is a reasonable assertion that, like many victims of domestic abuse, she was silenced while in that relationship. It is a sign of healing that Ms. McCandless was protecting her voice and perceptions by keeping them safe. Such behaviour indicates a sign of strength and resiliency, especially considering M's profession as a therapist.

It appears that during Ms. McCandless's teens, there were stretches of time when she refused to speak to her mother.

At fifteen, her parents paid for Ms. McCandless to attend theatre school. In retrospect, Ms. McCandless shared that the school's music teacher reminded her a bit of Bob Ross, only his mop of hair was carbon black and curlier. A happy memory, she recalls walking across the rehearsal stage of the concert hall, where a grand piano glistened under the lights. Sometimes when she envisions this scene, her music teacher wears a tuxedo with tails, which he ceremoniously sweeps aside as he claims his place at the piano bench. During the practising of scales, the client reports that her music teacher characterized her voice as powerful and perspicuous, as well as perfectly pitched.

Ms. McCandless was in her teens when her paternal aunt told her about the woman her father was in love with, a woman who was not the client's mother. Her aunt spoke nonchalantly and didn't consider whether the client gave consent to hearing about this betrayal of her mother or not. This family member didn't consider the impact this information would have on her vocal health and emotional well-being. Ms. McCandless was told that it was hard for her father being married to a woman he was unhappy to be with; that it was difficult for her dad being a Black man in a white man's world; and that it was the client's daughterly duty to protect and take care of him. "Don't tell your mother what I've told you," her aunt said. The client added this secret to the rest. Doctors misdiagnosed the occasional difficulties Ms. McCandless had with her breathing as asthma.

It is interesting to note that in her second year of university, Ms. McCandless thought she would become a speech and language pathologist. This perhaps is representative of someone trying to find their voice; although at the time, the client had no perception of same. She successfully took courses in psycholinguistics and attempted to memorize all class material before an exam. One of her professors wrote within her midterm-exam booklet, "characterize fully, yet succinctly. I like to read my novels while resting."

After her parents' separation, the client refused to speak with her father for almost two years. She states that her paternal grandmother attempted to act as an intermediary, but to no avail.

The client reports briefly seeing a psychiatrist by the name of Dr. Belker during her early twenties. Ms. McCandless met with Dr. Belker in his office weekly. The client states that she was there because of postpartum depression, or what she thought was postpartum depression, after her first daughter, Beth, was born. She conveys having panic attacks, with sensations of pressure on her chest and constrictions in her throat. Ms. McCandless recalls that married life was a struggle. She had returned to university to finish her bachelor of arts and bachelor of education degrees while working part-time as a waitress at a pancake restaurant. She reports that Dr. Belker's advice was to get used to it: "Things are the way they are." What she interpreted this as was: *Put up and shut up; accept your lot in life.* After that appointment, she didn't return, which indicates an awareness of being silenced and unheard. This is an encouraging anecdote, as it demonstrates that Ms. McCandless valued her voice and perceptions. It is unfortunate that her experience with Dr. Belker was invalidating and unhelpful. It is, however, fortunate that she did not let that experience deter her from seeking help at a later date.

Once Ms. McCandless resumed communication with her father, she would meet him every few weeks for breakfast at the motor inn with a buffet and a giant waterslide enclosed behind an expanse of glass looking onto the restaurant. She preferred meeting for brunch as the time was limited, which suited her fine because she was always anxious around her father and his unrealistic expectations of how she was supposed to look and who she was supposed to be. Sitting in a booth across from one another, the client confided to her father that she didn't know what to do. She was married to H at that time and he still had dreams of making a career as a blues musician out in Vancouver, which was problematic considering they were living in the middle of the country, in Winnipeg. The client took note as H spent his days writing out his daily itinerary, cataloguing photographs, and watching the O.J. Simpson trial in the dark of the basement rec room. From Ms. McCandless's perception, all the responsibility was on her, and she was having difficulty managing finances, a home, kids, and a career. She was too embarrassed to tell her father about the emotional abuse, or about the time H grabbed her arm and left bruises on her body. She was also ashamed to disclose his physical and emotional abuse toward her elder daughters, and how he believed that the baby she shared with him, Annabella, was attempting to manipulate him with her crying. Ms. McCandless acknowledged that she needed a way out but couldn't find one; that, in her words, she needed to be brave but wasn't there yet. She further acknowledged that H's threats to kill himself if she left him were another form of emotional abuse. That if he acted on his threat it would not be her fault; a realization that took time to take root. Each and every time, the client's father would tell her, "You're the matriarch in the family. You're a strong Black woman. You can handle this." This made the client reflect upon the question of how many other Black women are taught to be strong, to carry on in the face of adversity, and to suffer in silence.

As a teacher, Ms. McCandless also did storytelling in schools. Standing in front of an audience of four hundred students, she would share stories of fun and adventure as well as her love of the oral tradition. She reports having no difficulty projecting her voice or engaging with students.

When the client first met M, they would sit and talk for hours. With suitable therapy, Ms. McCandless now recognizes that her ex-husband was the one directing the conversation.

Supplementary material released to this examiner indicates that after she married M, Sundays became the client's weekly day of dread, especially the afternoons in which she sat across from him at the dining room table for what Ms. McCandless perceived as equal parts lecture and interrogation. The client became emotionally flooded when she disclosed that she was forced to listen to his airing of perceived grievances of what she had done wrong during the week, during the month, during the years that they'd lived together. M had told the client repeatedly and explicitly that he felt unheard, unloved, underappreciated. Ms. McCandless became an adept student after the passage of so much time. Over the years of living with M, she learned how to go quiet, understanding that a single comment uttered in her own defense would lead to days of being ignored or verbally attacked for being argumentative, self-centred, and disrespectful. Ms. McCandless reported feeling trapped and being fearful. Eventually, she would flee the table, run into the bathroom, and lock the door before turning on the shower to muffle the sound of her crying.

This ongoing tension manifested physically as pain in the client's jaw — according to Ms. McCandless, like someone was ramming an ice pick into her ears. It should be noted that the addition of a night guard and therapeutic Botox injections made to the jaw have greatly mitigated what has been diagnosed as TMJ, or temporomandibular joint disorder.

There is no question that the client's previous partner M exhibited behaviours that were abusive and detrimental to the client's emotional, psychological, and physical well-being. By continuously mentioning that she was the only person he had trouble communicating with and that he had friends, colleagues, clients, and acquaintances who had no trouble expressing themselves to him or being understood by him, he undermined her confidence. Just as deleterious was his proclamation that he had no problem making his thoughts known and understood during verbal communication with other people. He stressed multiple times that the person with the issues was Ms. McCandless. It was always Ms. McCandless. It would always be Ms. McCandless. It would be reasonable to strongly contest M's assessment of the client, as he had a vested interest in keeping her silent and under his control.

The client shares that M wanted to talk about talking, wanted to remind her of the terms of their agreement — the one he came up with many years ago. Under no circumstances was she ever to lie to him, and no matter what was going on in their lives and relationship, the two of them would talk. He insisted upon the rules being followed, even though Ms. McCandless reports that it made her feel like a child dealing with a strict and overbearing parent, with no time off for good behaviour.

Additionally, the client put her writing away for years, feeling the pressure of fulfilling his dreams, fearing that if she continued he would own that part of her, as well. It was a challenge from her eldest daughter, Beth, that led Ms. McCandless to pick up the pen and return to writing. "We have all this creativity and none of us are using it," Beth told her mother. Wanting to be a good role model, she decided to return to her writing. It would be accurate to state that a return to writing inevitably led to the reclaiming of the client's voice.

Toward the end of her relationship with M, there were months when the client would venture to speak with him at home only for her voice to catch in the back of her throat and stay there. It appears that the trauma caused physiological changes; i.e., the tightening and occasional muscle spasming of her throat and vocal cords. I would surmise that an additional mitigating factor would be the overall lack of use; that the rasp in Ms. McCandless's voice developed in part because she had limited people to converse with. The client notes the following fears in association with her former partner: the fear of saying the wrong thing and making him angry; the fear of being perceived as argumentative when asking a question; the fear of having her words misinterpreted and used against her; the fear of him filling in the blanks with ridicule. When Ms. McCandless did speak, the words tumbled out as a hoarse whisper, which supports her characterization of being silenced by an abusive partner.

The client reports that M constantly told her, "You can't ever just listen to my story. You can't ever do it. Right?"

Ms. McCandless reveals that in the months leading up to her separation from M, she started to secretly record conversations between herself and her husband. She states that the idea came from her ex, who often said that he wished he had a tape recorder so he could record their conversations and play them back to her as proof that she was incapable of hearing him correctly; incapable of conversational turn-taking; incapable of accepting responsibility for her actions; incapable of dealing with his perceptions of reality. Ms. McCandless further disclosed that she recorded these conversations so that they could be played privately at a later date in order to understand what it was that she was doing wrong. She shared some of the tapes with one of her recent therapists. At some point, the client's perspective shifted, and she began researching the terms *gaslighting*, *emotional abuse*, and *psychological abuse*.

An independent bookstore in Winnipeg offered Ms. McCandless access to a community classroom to practise her writing. Two years before she left M, the client signed up for one of their creative writing workshops. In the beginning, according to Ms. McCandless, M had no qualms about her taking classes. She postulates that perhaps this was because he still held out hope that one day his fantasy — one she did not share — would come true, that indeed, Ms. McCandless would become a famous author. He would become the partner of a famous author. The two of them would live together on the West Coast while she wrote and he continued to work as a therapist.

The client reports that the classes were with people from all walks of life who were keen to express themselves through creative writing. She states that she was amazed that people actually wanted her to share her thoughts and her words. It is worth noting that no one called her a horrible conversationalist. No one told Ms. McCandless that she didn't know how to listen, or that she was self-centred, or that it was always about her and her story. There was a shared kinship brought about by the love of language and the desire to express one's creative thoughts on the page. The client states that it was a revelation to know that her linguistic deficiencies had more to do with M than they did with her.

Signing up for workshops became Ms. McCandless's lifeline; they gave her something to look forward to in the bleak years before and after she left M to live on her own. They provided companionship, conversations, a celebration of self-expression, and the encouragement she needed to keep writing, to keep expressing herself vocally, and to keep living to face another day.

The client reports an incident when she and M were returning from a trip to France, lodging at one of the hotels near the Charles De Gaulle airport. Lying on the queen-sized bed, she was checking her emails when she scrolled down the list and noticed a message from a literary magazine on the West Coast. Opening the email, Ms. McCandless discovered that her short story "Whale Song" had been shortlisted for a fiction prize. It was the first short story she had ever written, let alone submitted. The client cried out in excitement as she told M the wonderful news. He asked what the prize money would be. She told him. "Well," he said, "you're going to have to make a lot more money than that if we're going to pay off the line of credit for this trip." Ms. McCandless didn't utter a word in response. It can be surmised that she responded in a way that kept her safe from additional harm.

Ever since Ms. McCandless read Eula Biss's "The Pain Scale" and Sierra Skye Gemma's "The Wrong Way," the client has wanted to write creative non-fiction. She reports having a drawer filled with unfinished drafts with no idea how to complete them. She had stories she wanted to share, but no safe way to write them without being triggered by the past. The client discovered a creative non-fiction workshop about working with outlier forms taught by a writer who has become, as Ms. McCandless stated, one of her writing besties. By all accounts, Nicole was a fantastic mentor and exposed the client to flash non-fiction, the lyric essay, the hermit crab, the collage. They were forms that made sense to Ms. McCandless and enabled the retelling of traumatic events that were stored in her brain as non-linear fragments.

## SUMMARY AND CLOSURE:

Ms. McCandless has engaged in music therapy upon my recommendation. Here are some observations since first assigned treatment.

"Who do you sing for?" Alice, the music therapist, asked as the client sat in a circle with a half-dozen people all keen to improve their singing voices. She's attending these sessions to work on the tightness in her throat, the muscle spasms that snag her voice like barbed wire. Unlike Alice's other clients, Ms. McCandless is not singing to an elderly spouse with dementia. She's not singing in a church choir; nor is she trying to strengthen her voice after vocal cords surgery. The client states that she was embarrassed by the question because, in truth, her answer would have been "the dog," which only serves to remind her of how isolated she became while living with M.

It should be noted that the mechanics of our voice are complex. They involve the vocal cords and larynx; the diaphragm, brain, and ears; our whole body; our mind, personality, emotions, and spirit. Ms. McCandless states that Alice wanted to know what she was doing to nurture and feed her spirit in order to move from silence to expressing her own needs. The client wishes she had an answer other than leaving a toxic and abusive relationship, so she made one up, hoping the idea of a face mask and bubble bath sounded sufficiently nurturing. Ms. McCandless has stated that she is working on incorporating self-care routines into her weekly schedule, a goal that I strenuously endorse.

The client is learning that reclaiming her voice is an ongoing process and that she has the right to speak out and speak up. It proves an uncomfortable notion for Ms. McCandless. She has been silenced for so long and even a year and a half after leaving M, her voice still feels restricted; she still feels like she's unable to breathe deep into her lungs, or to take enough big belly breaths to expand her diaphragm. The client confesses she is still keeping secrets like a beach ball held under water, the pressure at times so intense that Ms. McCandless is afraid she will no longer be able to hold it back. The client does, however, write in her notebook entitled *Listen to Your Art*, which is progress. After years of processing, it is clearer that M's self-serving rules, which have taken her years to understand, were not part of a healthy relationship and were, in truth, restrictions meant to control her.

The client had the opportunity to take part in a writing conference in Toronto. Ms. McCandless states that the conference's dining hall reminded her of Hogwarts: rows of long wooden tables, an extraordinarily high ceiling, oversized windows framing one side of the room. At the conference dinner, she waited for the cabaret to begin with Nicole, her mentor, and Eufemia, another talented writer whom she had become great friends with. Days earlier, they had encouraged Ms. McCandless to sign up for the cabaret, to put her name into the hat in hopes of being drawn and called up onstage. She'd decided, if selected, to read a passage from "Black and Blues," because while it was creative non-fiction, it was also lyrical, familiar, and something she could read with confidence. As names were called one by one, the client inwardly cringed — praying that her name wouldn't be announced. But then Ms. McCandless thought of M, whom her friends had recently christened Voldemort, and something inside her shifted. She began hoping her name would be selected. She wanted to push back against the silence that was meant to keep her small, contained, and under his control. When she heard her name, she was excited but also fearful; so many years had passed since she had performed in front of an audience. Allotted five minutes to read, she stood behind the podium, thankful to have something to hide behind. It was then that Ms. McCandless remembered the years she had performed as a storyteller in elementary schools; what it was like to have a gym filled with five- to twelve-year-olds held in rapt attention. How her voice was clear and projected loud enough for everyone to hear. The client channelled all of her anxiety into her right foot, tapping a rhythmic beat that only she was aware of. She began her reading buoyed by the beat of slam poetry and the supportive presence of her writing community and other writers who had become dear friends. It is unquestionable to conclude that writing rescued Ms. McCandless. It also reactivated her creative expression, encouraged the use of her voice, and gave her the opportunity to be a part of a community that furthered her opportunities for self-esteem and self-expression.

An Inventory of Wants and Needs

# HECTOR AVENUE

This 600-square-foot-home is suitable for a single person or couple. With two bedrooms, a remodelled kitchen and bath, and a petite but functional living room, this house is perfect for two people. The principal bedroom has sufficient dimensions to erect a number of bookcases; great for the bibliophile in the family. The oversized, partially fenced yard is well-suited for pets. Available as a month-to-month rental with

no damage deposit required, this gem is perfect for those looking for a more temporary housing solution. Bonus features include an excellent location, no references required, and we accept large dogs.

N  I meet with Donna in secret in her tiny office. She is a counsellor for victims of domestic abuse and works with people who have exited or are planning to exit a harmful relationship. I feel ashamed and guilty being there; as if the instances of abuse are inconsequential to my breaking M's rules. I am not supposed to leave him, and I'm not supposed to speak about what had happened, what was happening in our relationship — yet here I am speaking out after so many years of living together, fearful, isolated, and in silence. I understand that once I leave him, I can never go back because it wouldn't be safe to do so, not after my perceived betrayals and leaving the relationship in secret. With Donna's assistance, I make a safety plan for leaving.

N  Donna is also a POD, or protection order designate. This means that she can help me apply for a protection order, which would legally prevent him from having any future contact with me or my daughters. Even though I believe that I need one, I don't have the courage to apply to the court. I'm too afraid of his reaction to what he will perceive as an attack on his character and reputation.

W  We talk about housing options. I can temporarily reside in a domestic-abuse women's shelter, which will provide me with support from additional counsellors and from women who have left similar situations. But I can't bring my dog with me, and my adult daughter attending university will have to seek lodging elsewhere. Two things I am not prepared to have happen.

W  A helpful consideration, Donna suggests, is the SafePet Program, which provides temporary foster care for pets while domestic-abuse victims heal and get re-established. Given how much emotional support and comfort my dog gives me, I can't surrender him to the program. I wouldn't be able to stand the pain of separation while he is under a foster parent's care.

W And so begins the month-long quest on Kijiji, searching for suitable lodgings. When I find the listing on Hector Avenue, I apply right away and am rewarded with a rental contract as well as the keys to the house.

N In psychology classes at university, I learned about Abraham Maslow's hierarchy of needs, a theory which offers explanation as to what motivates an individual. The hierarchy consists of the following needs, from top to bottom: transcendence needs, aesthetic needs, cognitive needs, esteem needs, love and belonging needs, safety needs, physiological needs. Earlier models postulated that one level had to be completely satisfied before an individual could move up to the next stage. However, theorists today believe that our needs act in concert with one another rather than as distinct and sequential stages. It's not that I want to leave my home. It's that I have to; the tension is escalating, and for my own safety and sanity I need to get out.

N A month before the move, I confide in my daughters that I have to leave, which doesn't come as a big surprise to them. They've witnessed nights where I have slept on the couch. They've seen the tears, me in full-blown PTSD mode, his cutting remarks that he tries to hide beneath a brittle veneer of humour.

W Walking through a downtown department store on my way to get to my car after a counselling session, I spy a pumpkin-coloured couch and two queen-sized beds that are all on sale. With the emergency money I have saved up, I purchase the trio and schedule delivery a week before we will be officially moving into the tiny bungalow on Hector Avenue. I don't want my daughter and me to be sleeping on air mattresses or sitting on the floor of the living room.

N I gather important documents, small items, and clothing that I can transport to the bungalow on Hector Avenue. When M asks what I'm doing with all these boxes and garbage bags, I tell him that it's just an early start to spring cleaning and I'm just dropping the boxes off as a donation to a local thrift store that supports animal shelters. He believes this lie as I walk out the door knowing that I've just compounded one sin on top of another.

W The smell of paint overwhelms the small space as I roll Benjamin Moore Whitestone onto the interior walls. The colour is the same light blue-grey that I used on Coralberry Avenue. I thought that the paint colour would cheer me up. Instead, all it does is remind me that this isn't my home.

N The couch and chairs are delivered on a Saturday morning. Along with Annabella and my behemoth of a Bernese mountain dog, Toby, I will be permanently lodged in our new place within a few days.

N I hire movers to transport my belongings to the house on Hector Avenue.

N My daughters Annabella and Raven offer to help with the move. I rent a smaller-sized U-Haul truck for the afternoon of Wednesday, February 1, 2017, and cancel the movers.

W The day of the move I watch the clock, keeping tabs on M as he goes about his morning routine. He starts work at one in the afternoon and won't be done until the evening at seven. Since we're down to one car, I'm expected to drop him off and pick him up from work. The phone rings and his one o'clock cancels, followed by another call and another cancellation, his two o'clock.

I try not to panic as I keep my daughters apprised of the situation via text messages.

| |
|---|
| W |
| N |

I drive him to work. He doesn't look at me. He doesn't talk to me. He holds his backpack close to his chest and stares out the passenger's side window. I'm being punished. My latest transgression: wanting the two of us to see a marriage counsellor to review our relationship. I wanted to understand why it is so painful, why I am always the one at fault for all the fuck-ups in our marriage. I'm living in this strange dichotomy, some part of me still wanting to be in the relationship and the rest of me needing to be out. I feel the tension build in my jaw, like a turn of the screw tightening, as well as throbbing pain in my back and shoulders. His last words to me as I pull into his office parking lot: "I'm finished at seven and expect you to be on time. Do you hear what I'm telling you, Rowan? Do you understand what I'm saying?"

| |
|---|
| N |

A mad dash to pick up one of the smaller moving vans from U-Haul. A mad dash to pack and load up the van. My organized plan is quickly forgotten. I break down in tears. I ask for help loading random objects into the vehicle: the Christmas tree and ornaments, tubs of children's books, and an assortment of other things that seem so important to me at the time.

| |
|---|
| N |

Following Donna's advice, I take video throughout the house on Coralberry, thereby having proof of what is taken, what is left behind, and the condition of the house. I tack a note on a picture frame, letting him know that I have left and that my daughter and I won't be returning home.

N After we've unloaded the moving van at Hector Avenue, my daughters decide to go out for dinner. I decline their invitation and we hug our goodbyes at the door. I sit on the couch watching the dog pacing back and forth and panting from stress. I stare at the pile of boxes, the buffet cabinet, the green garbage bags tossed in the corner of the living room and think, *Oh my god, he will be furious when he finds out that I left him.*

# TEFLER STREET

At 1,000 square feet, this lovely little wartime bungalow is well-situated in the family-friendly neighbourhood of Wolseley. A block from the Avenue, it boasts a decent walkability score and is close to parks; organic, vegan markets; boutiques; and major shopping centres. This house has an updated kitchen and bath, hardwood floors, a separate living

and dining room, and an electric fireplace. With two bedrooms and a sunroom with newer windows, you'll find that this house has plenty of lifestyle to offer. A fenced backyard with a deck makes for perfect summer entertaining, and the single-car garage and separate parking are added bonuses.

N I never thought that I would be renting the house on Hector Avenue for five months. I thought that the house on Coralberry would be put up for sale and sold within a few months of my leaving. Maybe it's a good thing that I didn't know it was going to take two-plus years until he finally agreed to move out.

W I begin searching for a new home a few months after moving onto Hector Avenue. The house is too small, and I feel claustrophobic and sad living there. As soon as I see the ad for a house on Telfer Street, I call the contact person straight away and arrange for a viewing.

W When I arrive at Telfer, I immediately sense that this house will work for me and my family. While it's nowhere near as large as my home on Coralberry Avenue, it is large enough. The fenced-in yard will work well for my dog, and with a separate living room and dining room there is space to take my turn hosting the seven members of one of my local writers' groups.

N I don't underestimate what my fellow writers' group members have done for me. How I'm relearning trust, relearning who I am and how to let people in, relearning how to engage with the outside world in ways that are healthy. And even though it is difficult to talk to a large adult male about the house, it is made less so by the landlord's son's friendly nature. He appreciates that I can see the merits of the house — even though it is lacking a dishwasher, which gives pause to some potential renters.

W As a young woman in professional attire begins measuring room dimensions, I tell the landlord's son that I really want to rent the house. He suggests that I write a letter to his mother, letting her know how much I love the place on Telfer. He says his mother is a good judge of people and he thinks we will get along quite well.

W *Dear Alice, Your son suggested that I write you a letter to let you know how much I enjoyed viewing your house. It's a lovely home, one I can see myself and my daughter living in quite comfortably. As a former homeowner, I took great pride in my home. I promise to take equal care of your house on Telfer Street. I can envision my dog curled up by the fireplace; me creating a writing nook within the wonderful sunroom; my daughters and I gathered round the dining room table for special occasions. I hope that you will approve my application and that my family and I can begin making new memories on Telfer Street.*

N Alice draws her income from a number of houses that she rents out to tenants. I meet with her in her home; give her the letter that I wrote as well as a binder with information about myself and a pet resumé for Toby. We hit it off right away. She tells me about her health, her family. We drink tea and I meet her granddaughter, who has popped by to say hello. I sign a year's lease, hand over a damage as well as a pet deposit, and leave with brand new keys to the house on Telfer.

N Aside from having two ladder bookcases stolen and the manoeuvres that are required to get the pumpkin-spice couch through the front door, the move goes smoothly. Annabella and two of her friends provide the assistance I need. I pay them for their labour. It's kind of them to help and certainly much cheaper than hiring professionals, even if a few pieces of furniture suffer a couple of dings, bumps, and bruises.

N I try on tearful occasions to keep the windows closed. Just like on Hector Avenue, there are days when it is difficult for me to get out of bed. I can't seem to regulate my emotions. I'm either hibernating under my covers or wandering through the house bawling because nothing is settled with M, and I feel powerless, overwhelmed, and hopeless. I don't want the neighbours to know me like this, but I suspect by their *hello*s and *how are you doing*s that they have some idea as to what is going on.

| N | In September the house on Coralberry finally sells. The basement at Telfer becomes a repository for items held on to from the house. Whenever I walk downstairs to do the laundry, I try to avert my eyes from the pile of furniture and bins stacked like a game of Jenga. I am so tired of crying and being so easily pulled by the past.

| N | Beth and her family are visiting from Calgary. Annabella and Raven, along with Elle and Karina, Beth's best friends since high school, are sitting around the dining room table, nibbling on dainties and drinking wine. It's the first Winter Solstice celebration since I left M. Even with the new grandbaby in attendance, I can't shake the feeling that I've disappointed my daughters. I've lost our home; the one I put a down payment on, the one for which I am still paying the mortgage. I tell Beth I'm sorry as I rock four-month-old Gracie. "About what?" she asks. "We're not in our home for Solstice," I reply. "I've lost our home and I feel like I've let you all down." Beth looks at me. "Mom, home is wherever you are." I look toward Annabella and Raven laughing and in conversation with Elle and Karina. Take in Elle's daughters enjoying Christmas cartoons; my son-in-law, Jason, in conversation with Elle's and Karina's husbands. I look down at Gracie lying peacefully in my arms, and in that moment, I understand what my daughter is saying.

N | After nine months of living at the house on Telfer, I get a call from Alice's son. His mother has had a stroke, and although she is making gains, she will have to go into assisted-living care. Because of this, David lets me know, the family has decided to sell off all Alice's properties so she can have the best care possible. Time to prepare for another move.

# CORALBERRY AVENUE

This extensively renovated home located in the family-friendly neighbourhood of Garden City is 2,650 square feet. The basement is finished, and all appliances are included. Both front and back yards feature low-maintenance landscape. With three bedrooms up and one down, there is much to admire about this home. The finished rec room provides plenty of space for family members to spread out. The adjacent bedroom makes a perfect spot for sleeping while also providing a dedicated workspace for the writers and crafters in the family. The all-new fibreglass windows provide superior sound-dampening. New roofing was installed in 2016: a lovely charcoal that replaced the much-hated blue shingles the owner had been convinced to purchase from a sales rep. After seventeen years, she was glad to see those blue shingles go.

This spectacular home is priced to sell. Call now before one of the co-owners changes his mind!

N This will be my third move in two-and-a-half years, part of the semi-nomadic existence that I had no clue would be my life when Annabella and I packed up that U-Haul. After more than two years the house is finally sold. M has finally moved out, leaving me with the task of emptying out and cleaning up the place, all 2,650 square feet of finished space. Leaving me with six days in which to accomplish the task because Raven is scheduled, midweek, for surgery. I'm thankful that Beth has flown in from Calgary to help me. I'm thankful that my writer friends have rallied as well to help me with this Herculean task.

N After years of being M's partner, it's a new experience for me to ask for or accept help from others. With M, asking for help always came with strings attached. Having no community to call my own until recently, it has been a learning curve, this having trust in people, one that feels foreign, strange, and uncomfortable. M tried to convince me that people outside of our orbit of two would only want things from me and try to take advantage. It feels good to prove him wrong and to know that I have friends who've got my back as I do theirs.

W My daughter Beth is standing in the kitchen at the house on Coralberry. She's packing up glasses and coffee mugs. In the upper cabinets are rows of jars holding various gluten-free baking supplies that date back to before I left. "Do you really need these?" Beth asks, gesturing to the jars. "Yes," I tell her. "But where are you going to put them? What are you going to do with them?" I know she's right; that there's no room in the postage-stamp-sized kitchen of the house I'm renting on Telfer. I tell her that I need them and that I'll find room for them once we're finished packing up the house. I know it's not about the stuff I'm trying to hold on to per se; rather, it's about time. I need time — time to mourn and process the permanent loss of my home and what it means to me. But time is not a luxury I have in the current situation. Not with the new owners taking possession in a few days.

There is leftover food in the refrigerator, as well as expired items in the pantries and downstairs freezer. The house smells musty and closed in — a mausoleum that hasn't had its seal cracked open for over two years. I discover a dead mouse rotting under M's office desk and another one under the kitchen sink. Fur tumbleweeds still linger in the back of closets. The removed furnace filter is thick as a carpet with accumulated dust.

We open up the windows, trying to breathe new life into the house. I'm ashamed that my friends are seeing my home under such conditions. My home deserves better. I deserve better. Heather, who is petite and brave and writing a memoir about the recent loss of her husband to cancer, and who also runs a professional cleaning service and has offered to do the move-out cleaning as a gift to me, deserves better, too.

Bernie, whom I met through the community classroom and who gives the best hugs, and her delightful husband, Bill, are in the basement, dealing with the disaster of a tool room. The area is overflowing with boxes, hardware, mismatched lamps, containers of leftover paint, dodgy craft supplies, and various thrift-store finds. Tucked against the back wall is a dresser from my childhood, still waiting to be repainted and repurposed. They're tossing out anything that's dried up, rusted, missing pieces, or in disrepair; anything I won't use or that can't be donated. I'm fortunate to have their help, because if it were up to me, I'd be mulling over every paintbrush, every jar of mismatched nails, every piece of retro furniture waiting to be coated with milk paint. Every object tells a story, and I'm finding the letting go difficult.

W | I am afraid to let go of more. To feel more loss even if it's just the panini maker that I only used once.

N | I know people are trying to be helpful, but I want to make some decisions for myself. I need my family and friends to stop asking me "But where will you put it?" It's difficult for me to part with the detritus of my relationship with M. It's difficult to let go when other people are making the decision for me. But with only a few days until the new homeowners take possession, there isn't time to mourn and meditate over every tchotchke. I need their help. I appreciate everyone's help. If I were left to my own devices, who knows how long it would take me to pack up and empty out the house?

N | Somewhere deep down, I know that I am frustrated and angry about the entire situation; especially his abdication of any and all responsibility for getting the house prepped for the new owners; especially because this is time taken away from my visiting Raven in the hospital after her surgery. But I can't access it unless it's directed at myself. Anger is an emotion that still frightens me. I need to find ways to be angry with M and the situation and not myself. I work on envisioning Thor's hammer and giving M a mighty whack upside the head.

W | I schedule a moving sale. There is just too much stuff to contend with. Kathy and Yvonne, both wonderful writers, work on the basement rec room and craft room while I do a quick game of keep, donate, toss to help them out. In the laundry room, there's a clothes closet filled with coats and my youngest's stuffed animals from childhood. There are shelves with decor items that I switch out with the seasons and a clear garment bag containing three old wedding dresses I had picked up from thrift stores years earlier. I'd purchased them for the antique beading and appliqués, which I carefully removed and hand-stitched onto the wedding veil I made to accompany Beth's wedding dress. I don't pack up the three wedding dresses for donation; instead I bring them with me upstairs.

N  "If I had thought ahead, I could have picked up enough old wedding dresses for the lot of us to wear. We could have all been reiterations of Miss Havisham," I say to the gang. "How cool would that have been?" Everyone has a good laugh, me included. I head outside, onto the front porch, and drape the dresses overtop a tall metal headboard propped against the house with a sign that reads *Come on, Barbie. Let's get moving.*

N  I feel the tears coming on. "I just need a little alone time in the backyard," I say, shoving the grief down hard until I walk out the back door. Laughter transforms into tears as I sit on the cedar deck overlooking the swimming pool. Head bowed, my lower legs swaying in the warm water, I find myself pulled by an undertow of grief. I want to dive into the deep end, sit cross-legged at the bottom of the pool, and scream.

N  A note tucked into the back pocket of my jeans:

*Dear Rowan, I know this move is the most difficult one so far but I'm here to remind you that you've got this. You have not only the resiliency and strength and a health care team to offer their support, but you also have family and friends who are here to help you. And I know that having trust in people is difficult for you but look at how well you've done; look at the amazing people you now have in your life. And while you may be triggered, remember the skills that you have learned, like radical acceptance and distraction. You can handle this move. This is not the time to let loose the grief of losing your home. There will be plenty of time for that later. Just remember, I love you and you'll get through this.*

*Love you, kiddo.*

*Rowan*

*P.S. Stay hydrated. Take snack breaks and time outs as needed and ask for hugs as required. Hugs are a good thing. Also, laughter's pretty awesome, as well.*

N After the moving sale, I call a local charity to let them know that I still have a sizeable donation of furniture for them. They schedule two movers and a twenty-six-foot truck to swing by the house to collect the goods the next day.

N The movers from the local charity arrive and they are deep in conversation, debating the best name for God because *God* seems like such an unapproachable name. After some heated discussion, they finally settle on Bob. Bob is a name of an approachable god; someone you'd have no qualms heading out on a Friday night to the Legion with for a couple of drinks; a god who is all in for a convivial game of darts; the name of a god who won't use their omniscience to cheat at pool or cards. I can't help but chuckle, aspects of joy being in short supply these days. Still, it feels foreign to laugh; something I need to get used to, relearn, re-embrace and reclaim.

N They're efficient at their job. The taller of the two tells me to take pictures as the truck is loaded; proof that on the twentieth of September 2019, four days after I regained possession of what had once been my home, I donated half of its contents.

# MCMILLAN AVENUE

This extensively renovated 1,000 square foot main-floor duplex is perfectly situated in the Crescentwood neighbourhood. Close to buses, parks, boutiques, grocery stores, and numerous restaurants, the location is a walker's paradise. With a separate entrance and fenced-in yard, this home is perfect for pet owners. Please note that the house will have the occasional mouse scoot across the wood floors and that heating costs during winter will be higher than average due to the numerous oversized single-pane windows. Summers are a delight as you enjoy your deck and patio area, perhaps by sipping a glass of wine while listening to the many open-air concerts in the neighbourhood. The living room opens onto the dining room and kitchen, with unobstructed views from the front foyer to the family room at the back of the house. It's a shame that, unbeknownst to you, this architecturally designed two-bedroom will be scheduled to be torn down eighteen months after you sign the lease.

W   I'm fortunate to find a listing on Kijiji for a main-floor duplex on McMillan Avenue, right in the heart of Little Italy. It's one of those homes in Crescentwood I have long admired over the years. I contact the property manager, meet him with my well-organized rental binder and pet resumé, and sign the lease the next day.

W   With the contents of two households needing to be transported to the house on McMillan Avenue, I decide to hire professional movers. This will be the fourth move in three years and everyone is tired, including me.

W   I like the semi-industrial feel of my new place, and the location is perfect: central to shops, restaurants, my family doctor, my psychiatrist, and my nurse therapist, as well as my favourite independent bookstore. There's plenty of room at McMillan to spread out, and I set up a dedicated writing space next to the family room. It makes for a comfortable writing nook, although truth be told, I spend more time writing from bed or reclining on the sofa.

N   Sometimes I wonder if all of this stuff that I'm carting around, and that weighs me down, and that I don't have any use for, is a metaphor for my life. There are stacks of bins and sealed boxes, with contents I have no idea of, filling the enclosed side porch. The potential overwhelm from all the clutter does nothing but feed my anxiety or remind me of my house that is no longer a home. I need to let go of these possessions that are interfering with my healing.

W   I miss not having a home to call my own. I don't like the transitory lifestyle that comes from renting. I want to own my own home. I want to leave Winnipeg and all its painful memories behind. I envision moving out west to be closer to Beth and Jason and my grandbaby, Gracie, where I would live in a condo high up in the sky with plenty of space and light streaming through oversized windows and a spectacular view of the city. I dream about moving to the West Coast and living in a townhouse, the location of which would provide daily visits to walk along the shoreline of the Pacific Ocean. I consider buying a tiny house, plunked down in the middle of an old-growth forest. I fantasize about acquiring a compact motorhome and travelling the countryside with Toby, looking for that elusive place called home. All of which feels like a fool's errand. With no divorce in sight after three and a half years, I'm losing hope that it will ever happen.

N   Julian, the landlord, calls me in January to talk about renewing the lease. He asks if I'm interested in signing a six-month extension, as they plan on tearing the house down in July to build condominiums. If I had known that the duplex was going to be demolished and I'd be on the move again, I wouldn't have signed the lease in the first place. I hate the reality of housing insecurity that comes from being a renter.

W   Looking at the MLS listings online just seems punitive. I have to figure out a way to halt what feels like a compulsion that leads to no place good.

N   I sign the six-month lease to buy myself some time. Time to search the rental ads in order to find a place that will accept my ninety-five-pound dog. Time to sort through and pack belongings. Time to offer donations to a number of thrift stores in town. Time to hire movers and junk removers. Time to begin the whirlwind process of letting go of all the items that weigh me down, material things I haven't looked at since moving my possessions from Coralberry Avenue. It's time to let go and it's time to move on. Maybe during this time, the divorce will finally be settled and the proceeds of sale will be released. Maybe then I can look at the MLS listings without feeling hopeless. Maybe then, as my confidence and sense of community grow, M will take up less real estate in my brain. Maybe then I can find my way home.

## AN INVENTORY OF WANTS AND NEEDS

**Boldface**: items removed from home when I left on February 1, 2017.

*Italics*: items I hoped to retrieve from the house once it sold in September 2019.

Strikethrough: M's items.

*: daughter's belongings.

(d): donations to charity.

(w): wants.

(n): needs.

**Front Entry:**

- Black mat (d)
- Shoe trays (d)
- ~~His coats and shoes~~
- 1 chair — metal/micro-suede (d)
- ~~Painting — The Red Ensign~~
- ~~Guggenheim poster, framed~~
- Oversized clock (d)
- Oversized mirror (d)
- **Pie safe (w)**
- **Orange dresser\* (n)**
- **Black/metal chair (n)**
- **Black jewellery stand (w)**
- **Wooden Buddha (n)**
- **Bird candleholder (w)**
- **5 straw baskets (n)**
- **My books (n)**
- **Coats, shoes, boots\* (n)**
- **Toby's leashes (n)**
- **Toby's toys and basket (n)**
- **Toby's baby gate (n)**

## Living Room:

- 2 oversized metal lamps — brushed chrome with black fabric shades (d)
- Television wall mount (d)
- Apple TV (d)
- Micro stereo system (n)
- ~~Blue cube fabric chair~~
- ~~Beatles print~~
- Black/white Union Jack cushion (d)
- ~~2 grey metal/glass shelves~~
- Television wall mount (d)
- ~~Metal drum table~~
- Ikea CD holders — wall-mounted (d)
- Custom French pleat drapery — Ikea fabric — made by Rowan (d)
- Black/white rectangular graphic circles cushions (d)
- ~~His various books~~
- ~~His CDs~~
- ~~His DVDs~~
- Various decorative pillows (d)
- Custom French pleat drapery (d)
- Black microsuede sofa with ottoman (d)
- **2 retro thrift-store side tables (w)**
- *Surround sound stereo system (w)*
- *Panasonic television (w)*
- *Panasonic 3D glasses (w)*
- HDMI cords (w)
- **Orange vinyl thrift-store chair (n)**
- ~~3 grey rugs with underpad~~
- **1 thrift-store retro wood coffee table (n)**
- *Arco reproduction floor lamp with marble base (w)*
- ~~2 grey metal/glass shelves~~
- **Ceramic drum table (w)**
- **White throw (w)**
- **Orange throw (n)**
- **Marimekko cushion (w)**
- *2 orange sheepskin pillows (w)*
- **Button art — Queen (w)**
- *Metal deer statue (w)*
- *White vase (w)*
- *Owl print (w)*
- **White/black decorative plate (w)**
- **Table lamp — rectangular with linen shade (n)**
- *White ceramic bell-deer head (w)*
- *Metal moose statue (w)*
- **My books and decor magazines (n)**
- **My CDs and sci-fi DVDs (n)**

## Dining Room:

- *2 paintings, rust tones (w)*
- ~~1 framed print~~
- *White dining room table (w)*
- Custom French pleat drapery (d)
- *6 white retro chairs (n)*
- **Wood buffet (n)**
- **4 white vases (w)**
- *1 grey decorative plate (w)*

## Principal Bedroom:

- ~~Queen-sized antique-style metal bedframe/mattress/box spring~~
- ~~ObusForme mattress overlay~~
- 2 solid-wood dressers (d)
- 2 brass lamps (d)
- ~~Green vintage wooden chair~~
- White oak painted dresser with mirror (d)
- ~~1 wood/fabric-seat dining chair~~
- White closet storage drawers (n)
- ~~1 alarm clock~~
- ~~Bedding~~
- 2 sets charcoal pinstripe drapes (d)
- ~~His books stacked on the dresser~~
- ~~His clothing~~
- **Ladder desk and 2 ladder shelf units (n)**
- **My iPad and laptop (n)**
- **Pine wardrobe (n)**
- **4 wicker baskets (n)**
- **1 salt lamp (w)**
- **Bathroom scale (n)**
- **Vintage typewriter (n)**
- **"Oh! My God! I Miss You" print (w)**
- **My portrait at four years of age (w)**
- **Marimekko bedding (n)**
- **My clothing (n)**
- **My yoga pillow/mat and blocks (n)**
- **My books (n)**

## Hallway Closet:

- ~~Black/white poster of him at the beach~~
- ~~His photo albums~~
- **My photo albums (n)**

## M's Office:

- ~~His laptop and iPad~~
- ~~Painting of lake above file cabinet~~
- ~~His decor items~~
- L-shaped desk with hutch (d)
- ~~Filing cabinet~~
- ~~Bookshelf~~
- ~~Couch with ottoman~~
- ~~Espresso side table~~
- ~~Floor lamp~~
- ~~Art work — Victoria beach watercolour series~~
- ~~Antique watercolour of Saint Cyrus, Scotland~~
- ~~Frank Lloyd Wright clock~~
- ~~Banker's lamp~~
- ~~Camping equipment~~
- ~~Golf clubs~~
- ~~Sound-reduction machine~~

## Kitchen:

- Brabantia stainless garbage can (d)
- ~~Cordless phone~~
- Orange/stainless towel dispenser (w)
- Stainless microwave and ceramic plate (d)
- White and grey painted hutch with shelves (d)
- Pasta maker (d)
- Panini press (d)
- Toaster (d)
- ~~Electric kettle~~
- 6-drawer wicker coffee station (d)
- Stainless side-by-side refrigerator (d)
- Kenmore stainless stove (d)
- Dish rack and soap dispenser (d)
- ~~Water, wine, and margarita glasses~~
- Travel mugs (d)
- Gold/white place settings for 16 (d)
- ~~Modern cutlery, 2 full sets~~
- ~~Serving utensils~~
- ~~Coffee mugs~~
- ~~Frying pans~~
- ~~Porcelain place settings for 8~~
- ~~Espresso cups and saucers~~
- Attached knife/cutting board (d)
- Bread/cutting boards (d)
- Electric knife (d)
- ~~Knife stand — large~~
- Blue vase with ~~utensils~~ (w)
- *Grey/orange clock (n)*

- *Stainless steel slow cooker (n)*
- **Electric juicer\* (n)**
- **Stand mixer (n)**
- **Electric juicer (n)**
- *Electric skillet (n)*
- *My recipe binders (n)*
- *Baking supplies in glass jars with stainless steel lids (n)*
- **Orange salad bowl set (w)**
- *Wok (n)*
- *Stainless steel water bottles\**
- *White salad bowl (w)*
- *3 white platters (w)*
- ~~1 pot set~~
- *Orange and white coffee mugs (n)*
- *Orange glass jar lanterns (w)*

- *White ceramic tea pot (n)*
- *Toby's dog bowl stand with stainless bowls (n)*
- *Orange bulletin board (w)*
- *Vintage coffee/tea/flour/ sugar cans (w)*
- *Cookbooks (n)*
- *Cookie sheets, pie plates, muffin and cake tins, rolling pin, mixing bowls, vintage Pyrex (n)*
- *Goldenrod antique mixing bowl\**
- *4 white boxes/chalkboard fronts containing cookie cutters and baking utensils (w)*
- **Knife stand — small (n)**

**Annabella's Bedroom:**
- White painted desk (d)
- **Her clothing and personal belongings (n)**
- **Metal floor lamp (n)**
- ~~Painted metal bed — double with mattress and box spring~~
- **Dresser (n)**
- **Metal clothes stand (n)**
- **Mirror (n)**
- Green stool (d)

- **Silver metal/glass shelf (n)**
- ~~Bedding~~
- ~~Exercise ball~~
- *Bag with shoes and boots (n)*
- *Vintage light-up floor Santa (w)*
- Closet system (d)
- Her books (n)

**Rec Room:**

- ~~Panasonic television and DVD player~~
- ~~Portable record player~~
- Bar fridge — white (d)
- Oak coffee table with drawer (d)
- Oak side table with drawer (d)
- 1 sideboard — espresso (d)
- Floral fabric chair with ottoman (d)
- White kitchen table (d)
- White painted coffee table (d)
- 3 black/metal bar stools (d)
- ~~1 fully stocked bar — various liqueurs, liquor, wines, beer~~
- ~~Wine and bar glasses~~
- ~~Bar serving utensils~~
- ~~Phone~~
- Vintage hockey table (d)
- ~~His CDs, DVDs, and cassette tapes~~
- CD stand tower base (d)
- ~~His portrait poster at Victoria beach~~
- ~~4 dining chairs~~

- ~~Black bookcases~~
- ~~His National Geographics~~
- Exercise bike (d)
- ~~Micro-stereo system~~
- ~~Wolseley print~~
- *Teal drum table (w)*
- *3 wicker baskets (w)*
- Electric fireplace (d)
- Bar fridge — black* (d)
- 2 orange sofas (d)
- *1 multicoloured rug (w)*
- *Orange Buddha statue (w)*
- *Orange Buddha head (w)*
- Retro record stand (d)
- Retro green ceramic lamp (d)
- ~~Floor lamp~~
- *Cushions — miscellaneous teal/orange/blue (w)*
- *Suitcase table* (w)*
- *My design magazines — Dwell, Living Etc., House and Home, Atomic Ranch (n)*
- Mountain pottery vase (d)
- *Vintage wooden telephone (w)*

## Nook:

- ~~His vintage ice chest from cottage~~
- 2 white bookcases — melamine (d)
- Oversized black-framed mirror (d)
- 2 retro melamine side tables (d)
- Dresser* (d)
- Wooden shelves* (d)
- *2 cedar chests* (w)
- Metal trunks — one blue, one green/containing games* (d)
- Sunburst clock (d)
- 6 bulletin boards (d)
- Vintage hanging lamp (d)

## Craft Room:

- Purple star lamp (d)
- Futon (d)
- Black ottoman (d)
- Mesh garbage can (d)
- Bedding (d)
- Vintage wood desk and dresser (d)
- Damask rug (d)
- Black painted sideboard (d)
- Wooden file cabinet (d)
- Printer and printer supplies (d)
- Blue toolbox (d)
- *Vintage toy sewing machine (w)*
- *Moose statue (w)*
- *Sterling silver bowl (w)*
- *3 vintage needlepoints (w)*
- *1 orange retro planter (w)*
- *Blue glass Mason jars (w)*
- *Oval mirror (w)*
- *Vintage ornaments (w)*
- *Print of girl in rain (w)*
- *Wicker baskets containing craft and decoupage supplies (n)*
- *Black boxes contain craft supplies — staple guns/pens/markers/scissors/glue, etc. (n)*
- *Craft projector (n)*
- *Craft books (n)*
- *Fabrics and craft supplies (n)*
- *Jars of buttons (w)*
- *Desk lamps* (w)*
- *White scroll decor art (w)*
- *Vintage suitcases* (w)*
- *Black metal filing cabinet (n)*
- *Craft storage system (n)*

**Laundry Room:**

- Green ottoman* (d)
- Wooden chair (d)
- Swiffer (d)
- Stick vacuum (d)
- Metal garbage can (d)
- Laundry hampers (d)
- ~~Iron and ironing board~~
- Laundry baskets and drying rack (d)
- Microwave cart (d)
- Floor lamp (d)
- Green/blue wool rug (d)
- Front-loading washer and dryer (d)
- Antique mirror (d)
- Print of man holding baby (d)
- Cloth wardrobe (d)

- Freezer (d)
- His jazz print with singer who resembles you (d)
- *Vintage lamp — black (w)*
- *Coats and ski pants* (n)*
- *Plastic heavy-duty shelving (n)*
- *10 bins containing daughter's books and belongings (w)*
- *Vintage items on shelves — bread box, box of vintage cookie tins, baskets (w)*
- *Straw witch (n)*
- *Vintage iron wheel* (w)*
- *Canister vacuum (n)*
- *Electric floor mop (n)*
- *Steam rug cleaner (n)*

**Tool Room:**

- Saws (d)
- Shop-Vac (d)
- Ladder (d)
- Paint (d)
- ~~½ all screwdrivers, hammers, tape measures, levels~~
- Vintage lamps and lamp shades (d)
- Grey dresser with vintage knobs (d)
- Wooden sawhorse/table (d)

- *Sander (n)*
- *Drill and bits (n)*
- *Electric saw (n)*
- *Craft paints, stains, and paintbrushes (w)*
- *½ all screwdrivers, hammers, tape measures, levels (n)*
- *Vintage cooler (w)*
- *Hutch belonging to dining room buffet (w)*
- *Toby's puppy crate (n)*

- *Wooden shelving unit\* (n)*
- *Toby's crate (n)*
- *Christmas trees — green/ silver (w)*
- Rock Band\* (d)
- *Retro TV tables\* (w)*
- *Retro wicker tub chairs (w)*

**Furnace Room:**
- Quilt stand (d)
- Metal floor lamp (d)

**Cedar Closet:**
- Metal headboard (d)
- Laundry hamper (d)
- ~~His clothing~~
- Decor pillows and throws — indoors/outdoors (d)
- **Suitcases (n)**

**Shed:**
- His bicycle (d)
- ½ all hoses (d)
- Push mower (d)
- Push mower vintage (d)
- Wheelbarrow (d)
- Plastic lawn chairs (d)
- ½ all rakes (d)
- ½ all shovels (d)
- Dresser containing pool supplies (d)
- *Bicycle\* (w)*
- Cedar chest containing wood for firepit (d)
- *Gardening pots (w)*
- *Electric lawn mower (n)*
- *½ all hoses (n)*
- *Wheelbarrow (w)*
- *Winter tires (n)*
- *½ all rakes (n)*
- *½ all shovels (n)*
- *Garden edger and garden supplies (w)*

**Tea House:**
- 4 side tables (d)
- ~~4-piece wooden outdoor furniture~~
- 2 4-foot-by-4-foot ottomans (d)
- 1 wooden lounge chair — grey (d)
- 2 white lounge chairs (d)
- 1 wooden cedar chest containing pool toys/supplies (d)

- 1 stereo system (d)
- 1 firepit (d)
- ~~Stainless steel barbecue and BBQ brush set~~
- *Picnic table and 2 benches (w)*

- *1 wooden lounge chair — grey (w)*
- 1 black pot with artificial pine tree (d)
- *Wind chimes (w)*
- *1 oversized metal planter (w)*

## Acknowledgements

I'd like to acknowledge a number of people with Dundurn Press, who brought such enthusiasm, creativity, collaboration and thoughtful consideration towards the publication of *Persephone's Children*. I'm grateful to each and every one of you. My heartfelt thanks for bringing my vision of *Persephone's Children* to life.

Editorial: Jenny McWha (project editor), Melissa Kawaguchi (editorial assistant), Elena Radic (managing editor), Kathryn Lane (associate publisher), Whitney French (acquisitions and substantive editor).

Design: Laura Boyle (cover designer), Sophie Paas-Lang (interior designer).

Marketing and publicity: Heather Wood (publicist), Lisa-Marie Smith (director of sales and marketing), Kendra Martin (sales and marketing manager), Maria Zuppardi (marketing coordinator).

Freelance editors: Susan Fitzgerald (copy editor); Rachel Spence (proofreader).

I'm indebted to Whitney French who believed in me, in my writing, and in *Persephone's Children*. My heartfelt thanks, Lil Sis, for your wisdom and insight. Without you, *Persephone's Children* would not be the book that it is.

My heartfelt thanks to the wonderfully talented Tessa Vallittu, who created the botanical illustrations in "Forest, Tree, Branch, Root," as well as the strength key in "Revolving Doors."

My deepest thanks to my daughters, who set me on this creative path; little did I know what would transpire when I picked up that pen five years ago and began to write again. You've been with me every step of the way, both in life and in bringing this book to fruition. I am honoured and blessed to be your mom.

My thanks and deep gratitude to the land that sustains me. I acknowledge that I live and write from Treaty 1 territory, the ancestral and traditional homeland of the Anishinaabeg, Cree, Dakota, Dene, Métis, and Oji-Cree Nations.

My thanks to those unnamed ancestors, the ones who gifted me with strength and resiliency. I would not be here without your fortitude and courage.

To my grandmother Daisy. You taught me the importance of being a storyteller; the importance of remembering a history not taught in schools. Not once have I ever doubted that you and Grandpa Lever loved me.

Many thanks to Donna Byard Sealey, author of *Colored Zion: The History of Zion Baptist Church and the Black Community of Truro, Nova Scotia.* Your book gave me a glimpse into my Nova Scotian roots. For that, I am eternally grateful.

I am fortunate to have had the brilliant Chelene Knight as a mentor. A number of essays included in the book were generated in her workshop. Thank you for your generosity in reading and critiquing my work. To Chelene and my Advanced Memoir Workshop cohort, Deborah Elderhorst, Sierra Skye Gemma, Maggie Jansen, Mridula Morgan, and Dr. Farah N. Mawani, inspirational women all, thank you for your feedback and your friendship.

To Nicole Breit, a fabulous mentor, writer, and friend, words cannot express my deep appreciation. I was searching for a way to write my truth, and you were the North Star that guided my path. I am proud to call myself a CNF Outlier.

To the amazing Eufemia Fantetti, I'm honoured to call you my friend. Thanks for sharing your wisdom, your humour, and your incredible talent with me. Also, much thanks for your generous hospitality and the use of your pullout couch whenever I'm in Toronto.

To Rachel Thompson, thank you for the Lit Mag Love course. You demystified and taught me how to navigate the terrain of literary magazines. Like, Nicole, you've created a strong community of talented writers who support one another. *Persephone's Children* would not have been possible without you, my friend.

To Ayelet Tsabari, thank you for being such an amazing mentor. I'm most fortunate to be able to call you friend.

To Marjorie Anderson and Dave Williamson, my eternal thanks for your creative writing classes at McNally's and for your mentorship, friendship, and encouragement to submit my work. My first publications were generated in your fantastic workshops.

My thanks to The Writer's Studio at Simon Fraser University and to my mentors Jen Sookfong Lee, Christopher Fuller, Kayla Czaga, Claudia Cornwall, Eileen Cook, and Stella Harvey. Jen Sookfong Lee, your support and encouragement helped to keep me writing through many a challenging time. Thank you. Thank you. Thank you.

A huge shout out to my fellow Lit Mag Lovelies, Sparks, and CNF Outliers, including Angele Foley and Heather Diamond.

Much thanks to my accountability group, Shirley Harshenin, Yolande House, Tamara Jong, Hege Jakobsen Lepri, Margaret Nowaczyk, and Sharon Wexler, amazing writers all. We've celebrated one another's successes, commiserated over the sting of rejections, given support through the tough times, and formed a bond of friendship which I am eternally grateful to be a part of.

To my talented CWX crew, Jeff Franz-Lien, Yvonne Kyle, Linda Lafontaine, Deb Miller, Leigh Anne Shafer, Sheila Toews, and Matt Wiebe, you've been with me since the beginning of this writing journey. I am fortunate to know each and every one of you. Tami, welcome aboard!

To my Winnipeg writing group, Bernie, Kathy French, Heather Ginter, Linda Romanetz, Karla Weir, and Rose Young, you believed in me and my writing even through the difficult hurdles that I had to face. I treasure your friendship and our monthly get-togethers.

To my wonderful writing community, as always, we do this together.

To the amazing editors who have published my fiction and non-fiction, I'm honoured to have worked with each and every one of you. My thanks for your assistance in elevating my work.

"A Map of the World" appeared in *Room* magazine, Chelene Knight, editor.

"Blood Tithes: A Primer" appeared in the *Fiddlehead*, Alicia Elliot, editor.

A version of "Practical Magick" appeared in *A Harp in the Stars*, Randon Billings Noble, editor, published by University of Nebraska Press.

"Found Objects" appeared in *The Malahat Review*, Iain Higgins, editor.

"Hunger Games: A Quiz" appeared in *Black Writers Matter*, Whitney French, editor, published by University of Regina Press.

Domestic abuse, also known as intimate partner violence, is a tragedy that effects many women in Canada. Statistically, 70% of domestic violence incidents in Canada go unreported to the police. In Winnipeg, my thanks to A Woman's Place domestic violence support and legal services, Bravestone Centre, the Fort Garry Women's Resource Centre, Klinic Crisis Line, Klinic Sexual Assault Crisis Line, and Willow Place crisis line and shelter.

# References and Works Cited

"Advertisements." *Nova Scotia Gazette and Weekly Chronicle*, May 30, 1752. Nova Scotia Archives microfilm no. 8152.

"Advertisements." *Nova Scotia Gazette and Weekly Chronicle*, September 1, 1772. Nova Scotia Archives microfilm no. 8152.

Angelou, Maya. *I Know Why the Caged Bird Sings*. New York: Bantam, 1993.

Bachelard, Gaston. *The Poetics of Space*. New York: Penguin Books, 2014.

Cep, Casey. "The Allure of the Map." *New Yorker*, January 22, 2014. newyorker.com/books/page-turner/the-allure-of-the-map.

Cherry, Kendra. "The Color Psychology of Orange." Last modified October 6, 2019. verywellmind.com/the-color-psychology-of-orange-2795818.

Chireau, Yvonne Patricia. "Conjure and Christianity in the 19th Century: Religious Elements in African American Magic." *Religion and American Culture* 7, no. 2 (Summer 1997): 225–46.

Coates, Ta-Nehisi. *Between the World and Me*. New York: Spiegel & Grau, 2015.

Didion, Joan. *Slouching Towards Bethlehem*. New York: Farrar, Straus and Giroux, 2008.

Du Bois, W.E.B. *The Souls of Black Folk*. New York: Signet Classics, 2012.

*Fourth Census of Canada 1901: Instructions to Chief Officers, Commissioners, and Enumerators*. Ottawa: Government Printing Bureau, 1901.

"KKK Plan to Organize in Truro in Early August." *Truro Daily News*, August 3, 1932.

"Klan Took Oakville Girl from Negro Home: Hooded Ordered Foils Black-White Romance." *Toronto Daily Star*, March 1, 1930.

"Ku Klux Klan Have Organized Town of Truro Branch." *Truro Daily News*, August 10, 1932.

Macdonald, Sir John A. House of Commons debate, May 4, 1885. *Official Report of the Debates of the House of Commons of the Dominion of Canada* 18: 1589.

"Mark Rothko, *No.5/No. 22*." Gallery label from *Focus: Ad Reinhardt and Mark Rothko*. Museum of Modern Art, 2008. moma.org/collection/works/80566.

Matas, David. "Racism in Canadian Immigration Policy — Part One: History." *Refuge* 5, no. 2 (1985): 8–9.

"Orange Is Red Brought Nearer to Humanity by Yellow: Ricardo Alcaide, Ruben Brulat, Alberto Casari, Valentino Cortazar, James Hillman, Wassily Kandinsky, Christabel Mcgreevy, Allegra Pacheco, Gt Pellizzi, Mattea Perrotta." Lamb Arts, 2018. Press release. lamb-arts.com/exhibitions/48/press_release_text/.

Rich, Adrienne. *Collected Poems: 1950–2012*. New York: W.W. Norton & Company, 1973.

*Sixth Census of Canada 1921: Instructions to Commissioners and Enumerators*. Ottawa: Government Printing Bureau, 1921.

*United States of America, Census Slave Schedule, Sumter County, South Carolina 1860*. National Archives and Records Administration microfilm series M653, roll 1238, page no. 133.

## Credits

## About the Author

Rowan McCandless lives and writes from Winnipeg, which is located on Treaty 1 territory, the ancestral and traditional homeland of the Anishinaabeg, Cree, Dakota, Dene, Métis, and Oji-Cree Nations. Coming from a long line of storytellers, Rowan remembers sitting around her paternal grandmother's kitchen table and listening to her grandmother weave family stories or tales about her years growing up in Nova Scotia. Being Black and biracial, the daughter of multiple diasporas, Rowan wants to give voice to the experience of people living in the margins, navigating between worlds, ideas and ideals, and the social construct called race. Her creative non-fiction embraces social justice and celebrates hybridity as a way into story. A tangential thinker, innovative forms fit the way she catalogues and understands the world, and she is proud to be a creative outlier, weaving lyricism, humour, and emotional honesty with traditional literary techniques and subversive forms. When she is not writing, Rowan likes to spend time with family, friends, and her behemoth of a Bernese mountain dog named Toby. She enjoys cooking vegan dishes, gardening, graffiti, and fibre art.